MY SEVEN SONS

AND HOW WE RAISED EACH OTHER

DON DIAMONT

Star of *The Bold and the Beautiful*

MY SEVEN SONS

AND HOW WE RAISED EACH OTHER

(They Only Drive Me Crazy 30% of the Time)

CENTER
STREET®

NEW YORK   NASHVILLE

Center Street
Hachette Book Group
1290 Avenue of the Americas, New York, NY 10104
centerstreet.com
twitter.com/centerstreet

First Edition: May 2018

Center Street is a division of Hachette Book Group, Inc. The Center Street name and logo are trademarks of Hachette Book Group, Inc.

The publisher is not responsible for websites (or their content) that are not owned by the publisher.

Library of Congress Cataloging-in-Publication Data has been applied for.

ISBNs: 978-1-4555-6891-8 (hardcover) 978-1-4555-6890-1 (ebook)

Printed in the United States of America

LSC-C

10 9 8 7 6 5 4 3 2 1

To my wife, Cindy, (Shu Shu), and my boys, Lauren, Sasha, Alexander, Luca, Anton, Davis, and Drew. You are the air that I breathe, my heartbeat, the reason that anything—and everything—matters.

CONTENTS

⁣⁣

INTRODUCTION

IIIIIIIIIIIIIIIIIIIIIIIIIIIIIIIIIIIIIIIIIIIIIIIIIIIIIIIIIIIIIIIIIIIIIIIIIIIIIIIIIIIIIIIIIIIIIIIIIIIIIIIIIIIIIIII

At times, being the father of my gang is extraordinarily ordinary. Breakfast is served. School lunches are packed. Nobody's perfect, but everybody tries. A solid work ethic is essential to football, photo shoots, and everything in between. Mistakes are made and lessons are learned, sometimes the hard way. Ego trips and drama are left outside the door with a giant pile of muddy sneakers. There's no room on our schedule for Hollywood vanity. You don't want to know about the sights, sounds, and smells that permeate a house of seven boys.

"Eight boys," my wife Cindy corrects me. "You're the ringleader." She holds her own as the sole female in the Animal House.

Traditional, we are not. My four oldest sons, Lauren, Sasha, Alexander, and Luca, are the biological children of my first wife. I shared custody of them with her. The youngest two, Anton and Davis, arrived on the scene with Cindy Ambuehl, the love of my life. The last to join the brood, and the oldest, is my nephew Drew. Not too long after my sister Bette died suddenly at forty-two, Drew called and asked if he could come live with us.

Of course Cindy and I said yes, and we've raised him as one of our own ever since.

What the hell? What's one more kid? we thought.

You step up and do what's right, as my father would say.

When I was a kid, my father was not only my dad but also my best friend. Not an easy balance to strike, believe me. I've known plenty of guys who have trouble walking this line with their kids. They either try to come off as the Great Santini tough guy or like some sidekick who's just happy to be asked along. Walking in the middle of those two extremes is one of many lessons I learned from my dad—lessons that I now implement as a father myself.

My life has had more than its share of tragedy, and my family has been through painful periods. Still, I feel like the luckiest man in the world. I've been a soap opera star for over thirty years, the last eight on the most-watched daytime drama on the planet, *The Bold and the Beautiful*. I love my job. It has given me a life beyond my wildest dreams. And yet what I do for a living is a distant second to the love I have for my—very LARGE—family.

For most people, the 1950s television version of a perfect family doesn't exist. It certainly doesn't in my house. We live in a world where the very concept of family is constantly being redefined. In the best of circumstances, the crucial factor is love. Beyond that, you step up and deal with whatever life throws at you, and try to have some laughs. With seven boys, life throws you laughs about 70 percent of the time.

It's the other 30 percent of the time that you want to kill them.

MY SEVEN SONS
AND HOW WE RAISED EACH OTHER

‖‖‖

CHAPTER 1

Green Acres

During my senior year in high school, I was really screwing up. I just wanted to be done with it, and that was reflected in my academic performance. That motivated my dad to sit me down and initiate a conversation about my plans for the future.

"Donald, what's going on with you? You have to get your act together."

"Dad, I have no desire to go to college. I'm not meant to sit behind a desk. I have this thing. This quality that people respond to." That got an understandable "Hmmm" from Dad. I didn't convey it, or mean it, in a cocky way. It was the observation of a seventeen-year-old kid, borne out of my various interactions in the world with friends, girlfriends, teammates, coaches, administrators, and teachers. Now, my dad knew I had a big personality and was a bit of a clown, so possibly that "Hmmm" was him thinking sarcastically, "Really? Well maybe you should run away and join the circus." That might have been a fair comment in the moment, but he didn't say it.

I really did believe that my greatest assets were my personality and looks, and that I would do better out in the world making connections than behind a desk or in a classroom. But looking back, I have to admit that my strategy, or lack of one, was shaky at best.

My father tented his hands like a church steeple, which was always what he did when he was thinking.

"Well, I'm glad you have this thing," he said, fingertips tapping. "But you might want to think about coming up with a backup plan."

My dad was not a screamer, or a drinker, or even much of a disciplinarian, at least not for my usual screwups. He let my mom handle that. Most of the time, my dad was just my buddy. But if I screwed up significantly, then he would bring down the hammer. I don't mean physically, but he would get his point across without any ambiguity.

During our conversation, Dad made it clear that if I wasn't going to college, then I needed to pay for my car insurance and gas, and come up with my own pocket money. In other words, I'd better get a job while this nebulous "thing" was working out for me.

||||||||||||||||||||||||||||||

I loved my dad with a passion. I don't remember ever being mad at him. He respected my intellect and feelings. He never patronized me. Even when I was a kid, he spoke with me as though I was a worthwhile participant in the conversation.

But, above all, he made sure we laughed.

As a kid, I remember going to my father's office in the California Mart Building in downtown LA. He had an incredibly gregarious personality. He knew everybody in there, it seemed, and had a joke for each one of them. He had this cordless phone that he'd carry in the pocket of his jacket—this was years before cell phones—and he could click something on it, and the phone would begin to ring. One day, we were in the elevator with a few other people when Dad made the phone ring in his pocket. He pulled the receiver out and, nonchalantly, put it to his ear. "Honey, looks like I'm working late," he said. "I'm not going to be home for dinner." The people in the elevator stood there dumbfounded, and then began to laugh, as did I.

ıııııııııııııııııııııııııııı

When my father was growing up, he wanted to be a farmer. Not all that unusual except for the fact that he lived on Flatbush Avenue in Brooklyn. However, he explored his childhood yearnings in Hightstown, New Jersey, where he spent his summers with his cousins. He told my oldest sister, Elena, that when he milked the cows, he sometimes aimed the udder into his mouth and drank right from the tap. Later, he attended an agricultural college for a few semesters, but marriage and family would preempt his vision of life on Green Acres.

Though he would never actually fulfill his dream, for much

of his life he kept it right outside his car window. In the years before I was born, Dad worked as a traveling salesman. He sold a line of boys' clothing throughout the upper Midwest and was on the road for weeks at a time in Idaho, Montana, and South Dakota. While Dad was on the road, Mom, Elena, and, later, my brother Jack lived with my mom's parents in Lido Beach, Long Island. Although my father loved his family and missed them while he worked, the miles and miles of corn and wheat enthralled him. He told me stories about outrunning tornadoes and flipping his car over on a deserted country route. He also ran into anti-Semitism in America's heartland.

Elena tells this story about Dad from his traveling salesman days.

One Saturday evening he called on a customer at his home in very rural Wyoming. He mentioned that he was staying at a hotel in a nearby town.

"Nonsense," the customer's wife said. "You'll have dinner with us and stay for the night."

Later, when my father excused himself to go to bed, the woman asked what time she should wake him for church.

"I don't go to church," my father said. "I'm Jewish."

"Stop kidding, Albert," the woman said. "You don't have any horns."

Still, Dad was fond of the people of the Midwest, and his customers trusted him.

"Al, you write the order; we don't have to know," they'd tell him.

"You don't screw people over because you can only do it once," Dad would say. "It's not only unethical; it's stupid."

Albert Jack Feinberg, or AJ as I sometimes called him, was a good man, and his nature was to help others. Not too long ago my son Alexander and I went to visit Elena in New York. While we were there, we met an old neighbor of ours from when we lived on Long Island. Now in his eighties, the neighbor told us a story of a night when he and my father rode a Long Island Rail Road train home together from the city. It was snowing hard that night, and when they stepped off the train at the station, the neighbor saw that his car had a flat tire. "I was going to call AAA," he told us. "But your father said, 'Don't be silly.'" Dad then pulled off his sports coat, rolled up his sleeves, and changed the man's tire in the snow.

Though far from an overnight success, my father worked hard and was able to provide for his family. When I was born, we lived in a town called Long Beach on a barrier island off of Long Island. As the children's clothing line became more and more popular—and because Dad worked his butt off—he was able to buy my mother's dream house not far away in Lido Beach, a more affluent town. Even before my parents finished moving in the furniture, however, the company's executives called Dad into their central office in the Garment District in Manhattan.

The company that my father worked for was called Donmoor. The Isaacson brothers, three of them, owned Donmoor and treated Dad like a son. In the office that day, the Isaacsons offered my father a promotion to vice president in charge of sales on the West Coast. The company's Los Angeles office wasn't performing up to company expectations, and they wanted Dad to help turn it around.

Though Mom's dream house might have been in Lido Beach, when Dad told her about the job offer in California she couldn't pack fast enough. My mom was a sun worshipper. So when Dad asked if she wanted to live in San Fernando Valley or on the West Side of LA, Mom asked, "Where is it warmest?"

I was three years old when we moved from Long Island to California. I grew up in a ranch-style house in Sherman Oaks at the end of a private drive and on the slope of a hill that overlooked the whole San Fernando Valley. My father was great at working with his hands, a gift that he did not pass on to me. Even the most mundane tasks with my dad were a show. He had beautiful handwriting. And watching him eat was like watching artistry: the way he cut his food, and the way he never left a thing on his plate.

Dad could fix anything and loved to work with wood. He put up the paneling and molding in our house and built a gazebo in the backyard. He had a green thumb, too, which was not included in the genetic makeup he passed down, either. He planted the whole hillside around our house with fir tree saplings so the roots would hold the soil. Maybe his crowning achievement was a jacaranda tree that grew from a hole right in the middle of the patio. Each spring, the jacaranda would bloom in the most beautiful purple flowers.

||||||||||||||||||||||||||||||||

My dad always drove Caddies or Lincolns. I'd wait for him to wheel the big boats into our cul-de-sac and then up the rise into our driveway. When I was in Little League, I'd meet him with our baseball gloves. Dad would roll up his sleeves, grab the catcher's mitt—which I still have—and I'd pitch to him until Mom called us in for dinner. He'd never take off his tie—I used to think he wore it to bed with his pajamas. In my memory, his tie is flipped over a shoulder as he squats in a catcher's position. I don't remember him ever saying that he was too tired or didn't feel like having a catch that night. I think he would have let me pitch to him until the sun went down if I wanted.

AJ was a very gregarious guy and would make the dumbest puns and pull adolescent pranks. But coming from him they were hilarious. Dad was the king of malapropisms and would say things like "the whole famdamly." Or we'd all be riding in his car and he'd fart, then lock the window.

Dad sometimes called me "Deeb." My middle name is Bruce, and Deeb is a sort of mashed-up version of my initials, DB. Sometimes he'd put a Jewish spin on it and call me De-bala. He'd walk into my room and say, "Deeb, pull my finger," then he'd fart, then turn around and leave. I was a willing participant in the ongoing fart jokes—it didn't skip a generation. The same goes on with my kids. You can just imagine what poor Cindy has to go through in a house filled with boys where the fart jokes are alive and well.

The reason I think he was so good at being both a friend and father was that he never lost touch with the kid he used to be. That's where our friendship formed: the kid in me and the kid in him. The same holds true for my boys and me. Cindy still says that I'm the biggest kid in the family.

|||||||||||||||||||||||||||||||||

One Saturday morning, just before my sixteenth birthday, Dad told me to jump in the Caddy, that we were going for a ride. I don't think there's a better bonding experience between a father and a son than just driving along together. I do it all the time with my kids. But on this day, the ride with my father was more special than usual. When he pulled into the Pontiac dealership, my eyes got big.

That he was about to buy a car for me didn't come as a complete surprise. He had bought a Volvo for my sister Bette (pronounced Betty, like Bette Davis), when she turned sixteen, four years earlier. Still, when I'd ask him when it was going to be my turn, he'd string me along.

"Maybe we should wait until you're eighteen," he would say, his eyes twinkling conspiratorially.

When we walked into the dealership, a gold 1979 Trans Am sat right in the center of the showroom floor. A couple of years before, a movie had come out called *Smokey and the Bandit* that starred my favorite actor, Burt Reynolds. It also featured a tricked-out black Trans Am. I liked the movie a lot and thought that Burt Reynolds was very cool. But I loved the car even more.

Dad, however, didn't have the same emotional attachment to *Smokey and the Bandit* and Burt Reynolds's Trans Am that I did. Besides, he had bought Bette a Volvo to keep her safe. With me, he knew the apple didn't fall far from the tree—Dad and I were both pretty aggressive drivers. AJ believed that having that much power in my hands would be dangerous. And he was right. Trans Am or no Trans Am, I could still feel my heart pump in my chest. For a kid anywhere, a first car is a massive occasion. For a kid growing up in LA, however, it's arguably the most important event of your life.

Back home, and now the proud owner of a brand-new 1978 burgundy Pontiac Firebird with burgundy wheels and a burgundy interior, I was in heaven. My best friend Duane and I meticulously applied pinstriping to the car, and I installed a Jensen stereo. The next time I rolled into the parking lot at Brentwood School, my high school, I did so with Michael Jackson's "Off the Wall" blaring from the speakers. Soon the car would be known, endearingly to some, and not so much to others, as the "disco mobile."

I'd like to tell you I treated the car with the utmost care for as long as I owned it. But if I did, I'd be lying. I rocketed around LA in the Bird like Mario Andretti, but without anything close to the Formula One legend's ability. Suffice it to say, I put myself in harm's way on more than one occasion. I did doughnuts on the street, burned rubber when lights turned green, and raced down Santa Monica Boulevard. There was one street near me that was exceptionally broad, and when it rained, water always gathered in one spot. I would hit the pool going full on, and then put the car into a 360-degree spin. I also remember driving in reverse at 50 miles per hour and then pulling the emergency brake, which sent the car into an 180-degree spin. It was the epitome of stupidity, and I'm lucky to be alive.

I did have my share of accidents, however, and I have a photo of my dad standing in front of a huge dent in my car and throwing money up in the air. The photo was for artistic purposes only. I paid for the repair.

||||||||||||||||||||||||||||

To succeed as the father of seven boys, you have to be tough. Sensitive as well, but tough. You have to know when to lay down the law, and you have to let them know that you're wise to the crap they constantly try to feed you. In retrospect, my dad should have come down harder on me. I kept my boys on a short leash when they started driving. I told them, "There is nothing you can do or think about doing behind the wheel that I haven't done." When my son Lauren rear-ended a car that was stopped at a red light, he insisted he wasn't texting. "So you just didn't see the huge yellow Hummer just sitting there?" I asked.

What I've learned is that love can come in various forms. Sometimes it's a hug, and sometimes it's a foot up an ass. Both actions originate from the same loving place.

In that regard, I had the greatest role model anyone could want. My dad rarely missed any of my games in high school and was, for the most part, the type of vocal fan most fathers are, except for this one occasion when I was playing basketball at Brentwood School. For some reason, the refs that night were calling a very uneven game. All the calls were going against us. It was so one-sided you would think they were wearing the other team's uniforms. Our coaches complained. Some of the people in the stands began to boo. Then, after one particularly egregious call, I heard the bellow of a familiar voice above all the rest.

"Let the kids play! Let them play the damn game!"

I had to look up, and yup, it was my dad.

"Call it both ways!"

My dad let the refs have it. And then they let *him* have it and threw him out of the gym.

"You're ejecting me?" AJ said indignantly on the way out. "You oughtta be ejected!"

The crowd applauded him. Even the coach gave my father a nod.

And that's the bar Dad set for me: When it comes to being there for your kids, sometimes you just have to get thrown out of the gym.

CHAPTER 2

Zoolander

M ost of the big moments in my life seem to have been scripted beforehand and appear to come out of nowhere. The path to my becoming an actor is a prime example of this. I certainly hadn't set my sights on acting. If I had a dream as a kid, it wasn't to be on the stage or screen but the hardwood floor. I played basketball incessantly. I spent hours and hours out in the driveway practicing. AJ even put up a spotlight so I could shoot at night. I would play Around the World or H.O.R.S.E. or some other shooting game with my dad when he came from work or on the weekends. Most of the time, however, it was just my imagination running away with me. I would play Jo Jo White or John Havlicek. And I wouldn't be me; I'd be Jerry West or Gale Goodrich or Oscar Robinson. I would throw the pass, catch the pass, and, of course, make the shot.

Though I was a multisport athlete and loved tennis and baseball, basketball was my passion. And I could play ball. Though I was getting attention from colleges, pursuing basketball beyond high school wasn't in my plans, and neither was a continuing academic education. College wasn't an option. I had ADD, and I don't mean that euphemistically. At that time, the diagnosis didn't exist. So, typically on my report card, the teacher would write, "easily distracted," or "Donald has trouble keeping focused," or "he relishes being the class clown." The truth was, I did try. But I just couldn't concentrate on my work. Fortunately, I found ways to compensate and get by. I got my high school diploma by the skin of my teeth and, once I did, I knew I wasn't going to spend another day in a classroom.

In hindsight, my father was correct in thinking that my "I've got this thing" strategy was a bit abstract, but I did have a sense of predestination in my life. People reacted to me in a positive way, and somehow I knew if I just followed my instincts, I'd be okay. Even in the classroom, for some reason, teachers would bend over backward to help me.

When I graduated from high school, I began working at the Nautilus gym in Encino. The job was a perfect fit. Along with basketball, tennis, and playing second base, I was into boxing and martial arts. On my days off from the gym, I'd head to the beach in the Firebird with my brother Jack. Girls abounded, and life at eighteen years old was pretty sweet.

Then one day I happened to be in Beverly Hills. I didn't go there often, and, for the life of me, I can't remember why I was there. What I do remember was the man who approached me and asked if I'd ever considered being a model.

I had done some modeling when I was a kid, runway shows for the big department stores in town. My dad had shown one of the buyers my picture, and he asked my father to ask me if I'd be interested in modeling the line.

That day in Beverly Hills was the third time someone approached me about modeling. Not too long before that, a guy came up to me when I was working at the gym in Encino and asked if I would be interested in modeling. I pretty much ignored him. But now, with another person showing interest, I started wondering: Maybe this was put in my path for a reason. When the man handed me his card and it said he was a scout for Elite Model Management, I had a feeling that "my thing" was about to pay off.

"Make sure you call me," he said as he walked away.

I did call, and when I went to see the Elite scout things began to happen very quickly. He set up a photo shoot for me with a young up-and-coming photographer by the name of Kal Yee. Just as an aside, Kal has gone on to be an internationally acclaimed fashion, celebrity, and fitness photographer. His magazine editorial and advertisement photography has appeared in *GQ, Harper's Bazaar, Vogue, Cosmopolitan, Playboy,* and *Vogue Hommes.* Additionally, he has shot over one hundred fitness magazine covers, including my 1987 *Men's Fitness* cover and story photos. At that point, I was on *The Young and the Restless,* and it was pretty cool that both of our careers had taken off. We maintained our friendship over the years, and in the spring of 2013, he shot my son Alexander's first modeling photos. It was pretty special that the photographer who shot my first modeling pictures in 1981 was shooting my son's first pictures thirty-two years later. I was there for the shoot and jumped in the frame at one point so Kal could take a shot of Alexander and me together. I'm glad I did, because it's a photo that Cindy loves, and Alexander and I cherish. Though Alexander was, of course, focused on football, he thought he could make some money modeling as opposed to having to get a "real job." Lol! In fact, on the strength of those photos, Alexander was signed to Wilhelmina's men's division, and quickly booked a couple of jobs. But just as quickly, modeling fell by the wayside for him. His senior season was approaching, and he gave his undivided attention to what he was passionate about: playing quarterback. That worked out well, given that he ended his high school football career as the LA City Offensive Player of the Year and was offered a full-ride scholarship to Indiana University.

Getting back to 1981, my first shoot with Kal launched my modeling career. And, I was told, if I wanted to take it to the next level, I needed to go to New York, and ultimately Europe, and do lots of editorial work (magazine advertisement) and build my book. So off to Manhattan I went!

I stayed with my uncle Bob, my dad's brother, and my cousin Nina. Not long after I arrived, Elite called me in to meet with modeling agents from France. They ran the men's division for Paris Planning and were choosing guys that they wanted to sign and bring to Paris. Well, they signed me. It was both exciting and intimidating. I had never even been to a sleepaway camp, never mind a trip to Europe, and now I was moving to Paris, France!

By early September 1981, everything seemed to be falling into place, just as I knew it would. Looking back, I may, in fact, have been manifesting my destiny. The successes I was accumulating reinforced my belief in myself, which I expressed in the conversation that I had with my dad. I wasn't meant to sit behind a desk. I don't mean this to sound conceited or cocky. I'd simply observed that I had a certain presence and way with people. It was an observation that I only shared with my dad.

My flight to Paris was on November 5, 1981. I was eighteen. My nineteenth birthday was just under two months away, on New Year's Eve. What I didn't know was that a life-altering encounter was going to take place before I ever set foot on the plane.

The agency booked me on an evening flight, and that afternoon I was in the driveway playing basketball with one of my best friends, Glenn (the Silkman) Rotner. I taught Glenn how to play basketball. He was a good athlete who excelled in other sports but had never played basketball. Early on he had his challenges on the court, so I gave him the nickname "Silkman" as a sarcastic comparison to Los Angeles Lakers forward Jamaal

Wilkes, who they called "Silk" because he was so smooth. Eventually, Glenn legitimized his nickname. He developed a very soft shot! We were playing one-on-one, and I'm sure I was kicking his ass, because I always did (lol), when my mom yelled at me from inside the house.

"Your brother's on the phone, and he wants to talk to you right away," she said.

On the phone, Jack was babbling on, telling me that he was with his friend Dennis and that they were visiting Dennis's former sister-in-law, who was the Countess Ilene Medecin, and I had to drive over right away and meet her. I told him I was playing basketball with Glenn, and I couldn't care less what she was the countess of, but Jack insisted that I had to come over because her husband was the mayor of Nice, and Nice is near Paris. Finally, I relented. That decision had a significant impact on my life, and specifically on my heart.

Glenn and I said our goodbyes. I was going to miss him. We were bros and hung out all the time. I didn't even change out of my basketball clothes. I was only going to meet the countess because my big brother insisted, and I wasn't out to impress anybody. I just jumped into my Firebird and headed to Beverly Hills. I stood in front of the door in my cut-off T-shirt and shorts and rang the bell. The door opened, and standing in front of me was one of the most naturally beautiful women I'd ever seen. It was an electric moment, and there was an instant chemistry between us.

"So what am I supposed to do now?" I asked. "Bow? Kiss your hand?"

"You," she said, "can do whatever you want."

"The countess's name was Ilene Graham Medecin, and her husband, Jacques Medecin, was indeed the mayor of Nice and had been for nearly twenty years. He was also a member of the French Parliament and was the former French secretary of state for tourism. His most important post, however, was the de facto godfather of the French Riviera. He pulled every savory (he authored a cookbook) and unsavory (he had many friends in the Mob) string that hung over the pearly-white sands of the Côte d'Azur. I wouldn't have cared if he was Vito Corleone himself. All I could see was Ilene. I would come to find out that she was in the early stages of a pregnancy. You know that saying, "love is blind"? Is it ever!

〰〰〰〰〰〰〰〰〰

Inside the home, we all engaged in conversation, and the talk was all about me going to Nice. Jacques and Ilene said they would show me around the French Riviera. Though everyone was talking, the only voice I heard was Ilene's. That evening, I was on a jet heading to Paris and couldn't stop thinking about this dynamic woman I had just met. That she was thirty-two, married to a public figure, and pregnant didn't faze me. Did I mention I had just turned nineteen? She had said that she and Jacques were staying in LA for another week before heading home. She gave me her number and told me what day to call her. You better believe I called her. It was expensive to talk between Paris and Nice, so she called me back, and we spoke for hours. She expressed that she hadn't stopped thinking about me either. Over the course of our conversation, it became apparent that there was trouble in her marriage with Jacques. She described him as being extremely controlling, manipulative, and insanely jealous. Okay, that might be a bit of a red flag, but why should it stop me? There was trouble both inside and outside their marriage. So much so, in the coming years, they would make headlines around the world. The good news for me was that Jacques was certain I was gay, so I was welcome to be their guest and visit Nice. Needless to say, that was a gross miscalculation on his part.

When I arrived at the mayor's residence, it could've been a scene right out of *The Graduate*. I wasn't quite Dustin Hoffman, but that's the idea.

With the French Riviera as our backdrop, Ilene and I launched into a true love affair that would last on and off for several years. And while there was an intense sexual attraction, our chemistry was born out of this profound connection. The fact that we were putting our lives at risk was of no consequence. It was like *Against All Odds*, the Jeff Bridges/Rachel Ward movie from the 1980s, or the miniseries *The Thorn Birds*. Of course, this was real life. I don't know if art imitates life, or life imitates art, but we were in it.

Running around behind Jacques's back was difficult enough, but it was about to get a lot more entangled. Ilene was pregnant. We knew from the timing that it wasn't mine, but nonetheless, our relationship went from the frying pan into the fire. Believe me, it got scorching. How hot? Well...TO BE CONTINUED. (Hey, I'm a soap opera star! What do you expect?)

The time I spent with Ilene in Nice was incredible, but I was miserable in Paris. I was living in a fleabag hotel in the red-light district surrounded by transvestite hookers on every corner with whom I maintained a nodding acquaintance. I'd say "Hi," and they would say, "Hi, free for you."

I desperately missed everything about home: my parents, my brother, my friends, my car, and the food, especially my favorite Chinese restaurant, Far East Terrace. My family went there every Sunday night religiously. I would often drive to the restaurant myself and pick up food to go. I also missed all the other creature comforts, not the least of which was my mom doing my laundry and making my bed. She wouldn't have it any other way. That's a Jewish mother for you! I was a homebody. I still am! Except now it's not unusual to find me making the kids' beds and doing laundry. What goes around comes around.

After spending the winter in Paris doing runway shows and photo shoots, it was on to Milan, which wasn't any better. In Milan, I'd go to dinner with my Italian agent, and then right back to the hotel, which was filled with models. I found it to be a pretty vacuous experience. By this time, I had realized that being a model in Europe wasn't what I wanted to be doing. I called my parents and said I was coming home. They were thrilled. And, just like that, the next day I was on a plane. I couldn't wait to get there! When I saw my dad and mom, I grinned from ear to ear. I loved my parents and missed them. We got in the car and went straight to, you guessed it, Far East Terrace. The next morning was Sunday, and my brother picked me up at the house, and it was off to the beach. Boy oh boy, was I happy!

Professionally, however, I wasn't sure what I was going to do. I entertained the thought of going into my brother's business. He owned a ladies' apparel manufacturing company. It was large-size and maternity wear. I entertained that thought for about a minute. Nothing against Jack, but it just wasn't my thing. After I was home for about two weeks, I started getting my bearings. I was confident that, professionally, something was going to reveal itself. It did.

I was in the kitchen getting something to eat when the phone rang. The man on the other end introduced himself as Tom Hahn and said he ran the men's division at Mary Webb Davis, a large modeling agency. He told me that my Paris agents sent him my zed card, a small version of a photo portfolio. He felt that I would work a lot, and asked if I would be interested in meeting with him at the agency. I said sure, and we set the appointment. I met with Tom and his partner, and the meeting went well. I signed with Mary Webb Davis, and I started working immediately. My life had taken the best possible turn. I was making $150 an hour, and I was living at home with my parents!

I did photo shoots for all the department stores, German catalogs, Japanese catalogs, and lots of other work. This was the era of Bruce Weber/Calvin Klein underwear ads. Bruce was a superstar photographer. Everybody was talking about his covers and editorial work for *GQ* magazine. *GQ* had become mainstream, and male models were becoming stars. If Bruce Weber, or one of the other *GQ* photographers, used you for an editorial spread, it would catapult your career. And if they chose you for the cover, you were golden. Back then Jeff Aquilon was the top male model in the world. He was on the water polo team at Pepperdine University when Bruce Weber found him and shot a legendary photo of him with his shirt off. Not only did that one shot launch Jeff's career, but it also put male models front and center in the industry. They were no longer just props for the female models. I'm giving you that historical perspective so that you understand that booking a shoot for *GQ* magazine at that time was a very BIG DEAL!

So, lo and behold, Bruce Weber had a casting call at the Shangri-La Hotel in Santa Monica. My agent, Tom, told me that Bruce wanted to see me and that he might or might not ask me to take my shirt off. I laughed. I don't remember much about the meeting, except that it was pretty quick (I may or may not have taken my shirt off). Then, a week or two later, I got the news:

They had booked me for a *GQ* shoot in Santa Fe, New Mexico. NICE!

But just as I thought my predestination was going along as I had planned, life threw me a curve.

They booked me for a job in Santa Fe. Everyone associated with the shoot stayed at the beautiful Rancho Encantado Hotel. Again, NICE. Although Bruce Weber wouldn't be behind the camera, acclaimed photographer Rico Puhlmann would be. There were a couple of other male models on the shoot, as well as Kathy Ireland, who was just starting out at the time. Later, Kathy and I would work together on a shoot for a jean company. As you undoubtedly know, Kathy would go on to become a super-model and *Sports Illustrated* swimsuit issue cover girl. Most impressively, she has become an extraordinarily accomplished businesswoman. In 1993, Kathy founded her brand marketing company, Kathy Ireland Worldwide, which made her one of the wealthiest former models in the world. I bump into her now and then, and it's always great to see her.

Back to the *GQ* shoot. There was only one problem, but a significant one. The art director was a jerk and required "his models" to do a lot of kowtowing and sucking up. Not my strong suit. I left that to the other guys. He was a condescending son of a bitch, and I simply wasn't having it. On the very first day of the shoot, he made a remark to me. I don't remember what he said, but I do remember what I said in response. We were shooting in this very woodsy area, and I told him that he looked like a little wood nymph. Hey, maybe I meant it as a compliment! (I didn't.) He didn't appreciate my description of him. Suffice it to say, that was my first and last day shooting. Just like that, I was off the shoot. Oh, well. I did have a lovely few days in Santa Fe and met Kathy Ireland.

I suppose my quip to the art director wasn't the best career move. But I wasn't going to put up with his need to belittle and degrade me. If my response meant that I was off that job, so be it. I impart the same mind-set to my kids. I tell them all the time to stand up for themselves. Do it in a respectful manner if the situation allows for it, but don't let anybody walk all over you.

When I got back to LA, my agents were dumbfounded. When I told them what happened, they responded with a combination of laughter and putting their heads in their hands. I told them not to worry about it. If Bruce Weber booked me for *GQ*, I would book something else. And that's exactly what happened. Among other jobs, I did a Gianfranco Ferre campaign with legendary photographer Herb Ritts.

IIIIIIIIIIIIIIIIIIIIIIIIIIIIII

By the time I turned twenty, everything seemed perfect. And in my life it was. But things weren't as rosy for my folks.

When Dad bought the car for me, I didn't give the outlay of money he made a second thought. Like many kids—mine, for instance—I believed my parents had an endless supply of money.

Why wouldn't I? We lived in a beautiful house in a nice neighborhood. I never wanted for anything. We were always going to the Dodgers and Lakers games and eating out at Far East Terrace. We drove there in a brand-new Fleetwood Cadillac.

Now, don't get me wrong. I was grateful that AJ bought me the car. And I told him that just about every day. I just didn't think it was a big financial sacrifice. And when he bought it for me, it probably wasn't.

But things had changed.

Dad came home one day, and I could tell by his expression that something was wrong. His job was a huge part of all of our lives. Growing up, I wore the previous year's Donmoor samples all of the time. Most of my parents' friends worked for the company. Many of our vacations, to Hawaii and Lake Tahoe, were also sales conferences and executive retreats for company vice presidents and other employees. For my dad, Donmoor was everything, the only job he ever knew. His job was his identity.

By the time I graduated from high school, he had been working for the company for thirty years. If Dad had his way, he would have worked there until he couldn't work anymore.

But Donmoor had been going through significant changes. The Isaacson brothers retired—all three at the same time—and they ceded the company to the son-in-law of one of the brothers, who sold Donmoor to people who had no allegiance to my father or any of the other longtime employees. The new ownership began to run the company into the ground and fire most of the senior people. When the ax fell on him, Dad was devastated. What made matters even worse, the company filed for bankruptcy, and in doing so abrogated their responsibility for employee pensions and other accrued benefits. My father had worked for the company for thirty years, and he was going to leave it with practically nothing.

iiiiiiiiiiiiiiiiiiiiiiiiiiiiii

AJ tried to rally from the setback. At first, he thought that he could make a go of it as a stockbroker. He'd dabbled a bit in stocks while he was working for Donmoor, enjoyed it, and although he never got rich from playing the market, he never got hurt too badly either. He studied for the broker's test, received his license, and worked for a while for Merrill Lynch. Though AJ was a great salesman, he wasn't keen on speculating with other people's money or even asking people for money to invest for them, and he certainly didn't like waking up at the ungodly hour of the market opening on the East Coast. His broker career ended pretty quickly.

Next, he went into manufacturing ladies' apparel, a business that was the brainchild of my brother Jack. Dad had a partner, a designer named Benita. They called the company AlberBene, a Frenchified version of both of their names. Benita knew how to run a business, but Dad didn't, and soon the partnership began to sour. My sister Elena would later tell me that Dad called her to ask if she thought it was a good idea for him to take a second mortgage out on the house to bail the business out.

"You know better than that," Elena told him.

Against her advice, he took the mortgage, and his financial difficulties grew.

One day, when we were all at my sister Bette's house, I was talking to my father on the front steps.

"Deeb," he said, his shoulders slumped, "I don't know what the hell I'm going to do."

The image of him from back then still breaks my heart.

"AJ, you have nothing to worry about," I said. "We're going to figure it out and do it together, and we'll be all fine."

In my heart, I believed I was going to back up my words. I just didn't know how.

CHAPTER 3

||||||||||||||||||||||||||||||||||||||||||||||||||||||||||||||||||||||||||||||||||||||||||||||||||||||||||||||||||||

So You Want to Be an Actor, Huh?

Almost until I became one, the thought of being an actor never entered my mind. In high school, I had no interest in doing plays or taking a drama class. I had no interest in theater. Now, if being a class clown was a hidden precursor to the acting bug, that's a different story. That still holds true today. I like to clown around on the set A LOT. Unless we're shooting some intense scenes, I do more comedy than serious daytime drama during rehearsal. And, to be honest, so do most of my castmates.

I enjoy joking around with the crew. They're on the set from early morning until we finish, which can be well into the night. They do the heavy lifting, so when I walk on the set, I feel like it's part of my job to have fun with everybody and keep it light. Now, not everyone appreciates my comedic tendencies. Back in the day, when Peter Bergman joined *The Young and The Rest-less* to take over the role of Jack Abbott, he was all business. His rehearsal performance and his shooting performance had the same intensity. I simply couldn't have that and was determined to help him remove the stick from his butt and bring him down to my level. I'm proud to say that I was more successful than not in that endeavor, and Peter and I shared many gut-wrenching laughs over the course of our time together on *Y&R*. Our characters were antagonists, and I was fortunate to have such an extraordinarily talented actor to work opposite. He is a wonderful guy, and I feel lucky to count him as one of my dearest friends.

So where was I? Oh yeah, acting. I had no interest in it whatsoever in high school. I was all about sports and girls. And not in that order. When I would ask my dad for money because I was going out with my girlfriend, he would inevitably say, "If you used your brains as much as your putz, you'd be in good shape." I think he spoke from experience. I found myself using the same line with Alexander when he was in high school. I laughed with my dad then, and still do when I reminisce about it today.

Even when I was modeling, the idea of being an actor never came into my mind. But that would change, and so would my life.

In the later spring of 1982, Ilene was back in Los Angeles, without Jacques, for the last few months of her pregnancy. She needed stability, and the unpredictable nature of her husband's personality made her very uncomfortable. Ilene was originally a California girl, and she wanted to be home with all that was familiar to her and made her feel safe: her family, her doctors, and, well, me. Allow me to point out the obvious. Ours was a very unusual situation. The connection we first felt hadn't wavered. I was very protective of Ilene, and even more so given the fact that she was pregnant. In fact, I was looking forward to the birth of her baby.

I always had an affinity for children, especially infants. I felt very comfortable around them. When my niece Alyssa was born, my late sister Bette and her husband Marvin were living with my parents while their house was being built. I would often feed, change, and bathe Alyssa. I think the best time you have with your infant children is when they're on the changing table. You clean them, dry them, put those great-smelling baby lotions on them, and get them cozy in their onesies and pajamas. It starts as a one-sided conversation, but soon they begin to coo, and then, before you know it, you're exchanging some dialogue. I cherished that period with all my kids. So the fact that Ilene was carrying a child didn't intimidate me at all. It seemed we spent every moment together. I even took her to her doctor's appointments. Ilene had scheduled phone calls with Jacques, but other than that, as crazy as it sounds, Ilene and I were the couple, not Ilene and Jacques.

One day, I was walking past a specialty store, and a life-size stuffed carousel horse was in the window. It was the perfect baby gift. I bought it on the spot and had it delivered to Ilene. She loved the gift and thought it was perfect in the baby's room. I guess I felt the toy horse would give me some presence in their lives when it was time for me to move aside. Of course, Ilene and I were in denial, and living in an alternate reality. We talked about Jacques coming in for the event of the birth in the abstract. He did fly in a few days before the baby's arrival, and there was nothing abstract about it. The world we had created for ourselves came crashing down. We were both heartbroken.

It wouldn't be the last time.

After Jacques's arrival, my contact with Ilene was pretty limited. Her daughter Sean was born on July 16, 1982. I knew Ilene had gone to the hospital to have the baby, and I was overjoyed when my phone rang that evening and I heard Ilene's voice on the other end of the line. She wanted me to come to the hospital, and I wanted to go. We were incredibly happy to see each other. After spending some time together, I went to see Sean. It was a pretty special feeling to look through that glass and see her for the first time. Mixed emotions? Yes, but the overriding feeling was the joy that she was here and healthy.

Jacques didn't stay in Los Angeles all that long. And when he left, Ilene and I fell back into that alternate reality, but now it was inhabited by the three of us: Sean, Ilene, and me. By October, Ilene had to go back to Nice. Again, heartbreaking. Many, many times my phone would ring in the middle of the night, and it would be Ilene calling me from various countries around the world where she was fulfilling her official duties as the first lady of the French Riviera. The calls went on for months. In the meantime, I would meet girls and go on dates. But the feelings I had for them paled in comparison to the ones I had for Ilene. For better or worse, the countess had my heart. It was a pretty tough situation for a nineteen-year-old.

Then Ilene came back to LA just after my twentieth birthday, and we were back at it again. It became almost routine. Ecstasy, heartbreak, ecstasy, heartbreak.

||||||||||||||||||||||||||||||

One day in LA, Ilene said to me: "I think you're an actor; you just don't know it yet." I don't remember how I responded the first time, but I do remember it wasn't the last time she mentioned acting to me. "I see how people respond to you," she would say, "and I think acting is your vehicle."

As it had been with my modeling, it took hearing Ilene telling me I should become an actor a few times before I realized that the universe was opening a door for me.

As it happened, one of the people who inhabited Ilene's world was a gentleman by the name of Marvin Hime. He was a jeweler in Beverly Hills and was friendly with an acting teacher named Nina Foch. Nina's career included prominent roles in the films *An American in Paris* and *The Ten Commandments*. She taught at the University of Southern California's film school and was considered the preeminent acting teacher in Los Angeles. Ilene talked to Marvin and he connected me to Nina.

In truth, I didn't see modeling as a lifelong career, and I saw this as an opportunity to make a change. Besides, I thought, what do Burt Reynolds, James Caan, Robert Conrad, and Michael Landon have that I don't have? What can I say? I was twenty and cocky. As it turns out, I'm glad I was. I would need every ounce of confidence to succeed as an actor.

I met Nina in her studio at her home in Benedict Canyon in Beverly Hills. Marvin gave me the heads-up that Nina didn't suffer fools lightly. He wasn't kidding. She came at me with both guns blazing.

"Why do you want to be an actor?!" she asked me. "It's a thankless business, and the chances of being a successful one are slim to none!" By the time she finished her little pep talk, telling me how horrible the profession was, how much rejection it involved, and how much of a long shot it was to make it in the business, I was ready to jump in with both feet. She challenged me, and I was up for the challenge. I didn't try to bullshit her by saying that I'd had a lifelong passion for being an actor. That wasn't the case, and I figured she would see through that line. So I told her that no aspect of the business intimidated me and that I felt I had some talent. I needed her to help me bring it out. She asked me some questions concerning my background and liked the fact that I was an athlete and had studied martial arts. She felt that adherence to preparation, the routine of training, and the ability to take instruction were as important in acting as they were in athletics. And so the next thing I knew, I had a monologue in my hand with instructions to learn it for the next day, when I would "put it up," as they say in the trade.

I did as instructed. I learned it, interpreted it as best I could, and performed it for Nina the next day. I'm sure I wasn't very good, but I think she was impressed that I had the balls to do it. She told me I had a long way to go, but felt there was something there. I would find out later that that was a big compliment coming from her. She told me she was going to forgo putting me in her beginners' class and instead put me straight into her advanced class. She said she had never done that before but was making an exception in my case. I didn't ask why. I just followed the path that she laid out for me. She gave me the class schedule, and another monologue to prepare.

"Your looks are going to be your biggest asset and your biggest curse," she said to me as I began to walk out of her studio. "It will get you in the door, and then you're going to have to work twice as hard to prove you can walk and chew gum. Casting directors and producers will have preconceived notions about you."

Ilene was thrilled. I did the monologue for her a number of times in preparation for that first advanced class, and she was very supportive. Whether it was warranted or not is another story. When I showed up for my first class, I recognized several of the people there. Broadway and film star Tovah Feldshuh; Annette Charles, who was Cha Cha in the movie *Grease*; and, of all people, John Bauman, better known as "Bowzer" from a popular singing group at the time named Sha Na Na. I felt like a fish out of water, and I'd be lying if I said I wasn't nervous. When my time came,

I took a deep breath and performed the monologue. Nina cri-
tiqued it, and though I don't remember exactly what she said, I do
remember feeling a sense of relief that it was over.

In the meantime, I was still working as a model for Mary
Webb Davis. My agent, Tom Hann, had a friend named Sid
Craig, who was a theatrical agent. One day, not long after I had
started classes with Nina, Sid stopped by Mary Webb to have
lunch with Tom, and he happened to see my picture on the wall.
"That's Don Diamont," Tom said to Sid. "He's got a lot of personality and confidence to match." As luck would have it, I came
walking in the door just then. Sid introduced himself and asked
if I would be willing to meet at his office and talk with him. I
said, "Sure, I'll talk to anybody."

As a general rule, models fall all over themselves if
approached by a theatrical agent. And, I guess, Tom and Sid
thought my response was cocky. But I have never fawned over
anyone. That was something I learned from my father and
passed on to my boys: No one is better than you.

At the end of my meeting with Sid, he asked me to come back
and do a scene for him. At that point, I had done one monologue
and one scene in Nina's advanced class. I asked the actress who I
had done the scene with if she would put it up with me for a theatrical agent. She was gracious enough to help me out.

Sid signed me right after we did the scene, and almost
immediately started sending me out on auditions. And, within
just a few weeks, I booked my first job. It was a film called *Go*

for the Gold. The stars were Oscar winner (and Laura Dern's father) Bruce Dern and Katherine Ross, of *Butch Cassidy and the Sundance Kid* fame. The talented actress Leslie Hope and I were the young leads. The former child star and veteran film and television actor Jackie Cooper was directing. I had auditioned for Jackie, and he was the one who booked me for the job. The film was being shot in Santa Barbara, and riding to the location that first day was a transformative moment for me. Growing up in Los Angeles, it was routine to see location trucks and Star Wagons on almost a daily basis. And where there were Star Wagons, there were stars. My mom would always slow down to try to catch a glimpse of one. This time I wasn't with my mom. I was in a transport van being driven to the location shoot. The closer we got, the faster my heart beat. It was quite an adrenaline rush. A production assistant led me to my dressing-room trailer, and then to the makeup trailer. When I stepped out of makeup, Jackie Cooper was standing there. He grabbed me and put me in a headlock. He said, "You're going to be a star, kid!" On the one hand, I felt like I had always known this would happen. On the other hand, I couldn't believe it was happening.

My mom was a big fan of Jackie Cooper, so of course I told her to come to the location with my sister. She was excited to see me on the set, but I think even more excited to meet Jackie. He was a guy's guy, and completely unaffected and unpretentious. He was as charming as could be with my mom and Bette. We all took pictures together. Mom was over the moon. She and Bette loved watching me shoot my first scene with Leslie, which was held on a beach in Santa Barbara in beautiful weather. My mom and sister sat in director's chairs next to Jackie. It was a perfect day! Just perfect.

Except it was show business perfect, which means it was anything but perfect.

That night, there were some rumblings about production problems, and the very next day *Go for the Gold* was shut down. Among other financial issues, the producer bounced a check to the Santa Barbara Police Department. Additionally, the documentation he'd given SAG to prove he had the money to pay the actors was fraudulent. Busted. Wait! What?! What happened to that "You're going to be a star, kid" thing??? One day I'm shooting on location having the time of my life, and the next I'm jobless and driving home. WELCOME TO SHOWBIZ! I was disappointed but undeterred. Just as with the *GQ* shoot, if I booked one good acting job, then I knew I would book another. *Go for the Gold* simply wasn't meant to be.

The path you take doesn't always go in a straight line, and that was the life lesson I was learning. There will be twists and turns. No wrong turns. Just detours. I tell my kids all the time, embrace and enjoy the journey. Sometimes the drive can be more fulfilling than the destination. Unless, and only unless, you're on the 405 freeway in Los Angeles.

Nothing is fulfilling there!

CHAPTER **4**

‖‖

Like Sands through the Hourglass

In the weeks after the *Go with the Gold* debacle, I booked a couple of small roles. One was a sleazy nightclub guy on a show called *Divorce Court* and another as an Elvis impersonator on *The Fall Guy*, a show that starred one of my childhood idols, Lee Majors from *The Six Million Dollar Man*.

Most actors who have any success at all in show business have a "turn on a dime" moment that they can recount for you. I know I did.

Around this time, the daytime drama *The Days of Our Lives* had begun conducting a search for a new character. During the late 1970s, *Days* had gone through a metamorphosis of sorts. As some of the mainstay characters on the drama became old and tired, ratings for the perennial daytime hit began to slip. By

1980, producers had orchestrated a wholesale turnover of characters with uneven success. One of the new characters, however, captured the fancy of the fans, and in doing so helped to save the show. That role was the torch singer Liz Chandler, played by Gloria Loring. By 1984, Gloria Loring was one of the most famous actors on daytime TV.

It's important to this part of my story to understand that daytime dramas in the mid-1980s were at the height of their popularity. These were the golden years of Luke and Laura, when soaps had fans like Elizabeth Taylor and Sammy Davis Jr., years before cable and the OJ trial—the first reality TV show—began to erode viewership. To give you an example of how popular soaps were back then, in her book about writing for soaps, Jean Rouverol recounts a story about a seminar with the cast of *General Hospital*, held at Harvard University in the early '80s. Students and fans of the show climbed fire escapes to get into the hall, and the mob grew so large and unruly that police were summoned to escort cast members out of the building. At Harvard!

〰〰〰〰〰〰〰〰

The part the producers on *Days* were trying to fill would create a love triangle with a character to come between the Liz Chandler and Dr. Neil Curtis relationship. When I was around seven years old, I loved cuddling up with my mom to nervously watch the Gothic soap opera *Dark Shadows*, along with its lead character, the vampire Barnabas Collins. That was the extent of my exposure to daytime dramas. So in the spring of 1984 when Sid sent me to *Days* to audition for the part, I knew little about soaps and nothing about Gloria Loring.

The character's name was Carlo Forenza, a monied South American revolutionary. I was set to screen-test Carlo with the show's star. When I first saw Gloria on the set, she had her back to me, and when she turned around I was like, wow! Being a soap actor wasn't going to be bad at all. I gave the scene all I had. I'd been an actor for all of about four months, dating back to the day I did my first monologue for Nina Foch. What I lacked in experience, however, I made up for with youthful confidence. Since Carlo was a South American, I wanted to play him with an accent. But they wouldn't let me. To be honest, I thought the character was an ill-conceived venture from the start.

"Don obviously felt he had nailed it," Gloria later said in a piece in *People* magazine, "because when he went out the door, he let out this scream like he had just won the Super Bowl."

A couple of days later, I was at the gym when my beeper went off. And yes, I did say "beeper." That's how long ago this took place. The number on display was Sid Craig's. I called from a pay phone, and he answered.

"Is this Carlo?" he asked.

"No," I said, "It's Donald."

What do you expect? I was twenty-one and at the gym. When it finally dawned on me that Sid meant Carlo Forenza, his way of telling me I got the job, I jumped straight up in the air and bolted out of the door. I had the Firebird floored all the way home. As I pulled into the cul-de-sac and up the driveway to the house, I was leaning on the horn. My parents came out of the front door.

"I got it!" I yelled. "I got the part."

My agent later told me that Doris Sabbah, the casting director, told him they had gone through an extensive casting and couldn't find the right guy. Right after I read for the part, Doris called Sid and said, "You sent me my Carlo." I was twenty-one years old, and that audition marked the beginning of a career in daytime dramas that would last my entire adult life!

I was thrilled to have landed the role. But I was equally happy to have the ability to help my dad and mom and give back a little of what they had given so freely to me. So much of what's right and what's wrong in life is shaded in gray. But when the right thing to do is crystal clear, you do it without question. I think that's as good a definition of maturity as any I've ever heard.

After I got the gig, one of the first things Jack and I did was buy my mom a new car. She'd been driving around in an old Caddy that was like a bucket of bolts. We got her an Oldsmobile with vanity plates that read: FRM DA BOYS.

‖‖‖‖‖‖‖‖‖‖‖‖‖‖‖‖‖‖‖‖‖

Though I was flying high, my lack of experience as an actor would bring things crashing down to earth. I wasn't just a little green; I was green all over. The first scene I had in *Days* had me interacting with all of these very accomplished stars of the show in a party. At some point, it dawned on me that this wasn't a basketball court. And there was no place to hide.

Al Rabin, the executive producer, didn't waste any time crawling up my butt. He was watching from the booth and immediately walked onto the soundstage and pulled me about ten feet off the set but within earshot of the cast. I'll never forget what he said. "I can take an actor who's nervous, but I can't take an actor without energy," he barked. "Now get it together!" That marked the beginning of the end of our relationship. He went out of his way to embarrass and humiliate me. To some extent, he accomplished both. I pulled up my big-boy pants, however, and walked back on the set.

Although Al's behavior was inexcusable, I have to take some of the blame. Up to this point, I hadn't seen acting as anything more than a business. A way to make money. I wasn't in it for the art. To that end, when I had my first sit-down with Al before my first day on the set, I naïvely thought I could talk to him about publicity as well as character development. I thought the two were equally important, and while I may have been accurate in that assumption, he wasn't the guy to talk to about publicity. He wanted me focused on learning my craft and not be concerned with self-promotion. He conveyed just that to me in our meeting. Still, if he felt he needed to reinforce that by hanging me out to dry in front of the cast on my first day of shooting, he made a mistake. From that moment on, I had no desire to cultivate his favor. Besides, I began to realize what being an actor means, and I was too competitive not to want to learn. Being successful was the only option.

Meanwhile, beautiful, talented women surrounded me. Within the first week of being on the show, I hooked up with a cast member who shall remain nameless. And a week after that, I went out to dinner with Gloria. We ate at a Japanese restaurant within walking distance of the studio and started making out before they served the miso soup. We were out of there and off to the Sheraton Universal Hotel. I don't think that was what Al Rabin had in mind for fleshing out my character.

<hr>

At the time, Gloria was thirty-six and on the last legs of her marriage to talk show host, and later *Growing Pains* star, Alan Thicke. Now they're both probably best known, and happily so, as Robin Thicke's parents. Within a short time of our involvement, Gloria filed for divorce from Al. She didn't divorce him for me, but the strength of our relationship, and how good she felt about herself in it, empowered her to put an official end to a bad situation. Gloria is an incredibly kind and loving soul. In spite of my feeling for Ilene, my relationship with Gloria was never a fling. We had strong feelings for each other and, from the beginning, were mutually surprised by them. We were in love and remained that way throughout our three-year relationship. In fact, we remain friends today.

At the time, I thought I had reconciled my feelings for Ilene and put our relationship in its proper perspective. I was kidding myself. Some months into my relationship with Gloria, Ilene came back to Los Angeles. She reached out to me, and I initially told her I couldn't be with her. The weekend following her return, I was with Gloria at her beach house in Malibu. She could see my mind was somewhere else. When she asked me what was wrong, I told her. She knew about my history with Ilene. I looked at Gloria and tearfully said, "I miss her." We talked about it that evening and went to bed. The next morning we both realized we needed some kind of resolution. It was painful for Gloria, but she showed the grace that defines her as a person. She didn't want to be with me if I was only halfway there. She didn't express it with hostility but, amazingly, with compassion.

So off I went to see Ilene. It's not easy being stuck between two beautiful, dynamic women. I'm not being sarcastic. I had very genuine feelings for Gloria and let Ilene know about them. I told her that if she didn't leave Jacques, I was going to commit to Gloria and not look back. My request was unrealistic, and part of me knew that. Ilene wasn't married to some average Joe. He was a very powerful, connected guy. We were probably both still alive because he had a particular code of what behavior he would allow or not allow. He told her that if she ever left him, he would have her killed. Suffice it to say, the Count de Medici who swept her off her feet was not all that he portrayed himself to be. And even if Ilene were somehow able to break free of Jacques, he would never let her take her daughter Sean. On top of all of that, leaving Jacques would mean throwing away the most prestigious part of her life: the position, the title, and the money. Would she sacrifice all of that for a twenty-one-year-old man just starting his adult life? The answer was no. She hated the fact that I had feelings for another woman. She wanted it both ways, but she knew that was unrealistic. And so I drove back to Gloria, sad, but content that the situation was resolved.

I would stay in touch with Ilene, and periodically we'd see each other over the years. But we would never again be what we once were. Ilene's life as King Jacques's queen of the French Riviera would eventually come to a dark and dramatic end. The people of France voted a socialist-leaning government into power, and they came after Jacques Medecin. When he found out he was going to be prosecuted on wide-ranging corruption charges, Jacques, Ilene, and Sean fled the country for asylum in Uruguay. Literally, under cover of darkness. Their marriage crumbled soon after, and the battle for custody of Sean ensued. Jacques ended up dropping dead from a massive heart attack. Ilene and Sean were able to move back to Los Angeles and get on with their lives, and today Ilene is happily married. Time heals all wounds.

Ilene and I remain dear friends. In fact, Cindy sold Ilene her Los Angeles home.

When I returned to Gloria, I let her know that I had ended things with Ilene. While she had some trepidation, ultimately my actions gave her all the reassurance she needed.

While all this drama was all going on, my day job was working on a soap opera. No doubt my executive producer was thrilled with my budding romance and all the press it was getting. NOT! In the meantime, I was trying to learn what the hell I was doing as an actor. To that end, Gloria was a tremendous help. She encouraged me to be fully present and engaged in a scene. To listen. Action, intention, motivation...

It was all part of the craft, and I was learning on the job. Keep in mind, this is daytime drama. You're talking about a tremendous amount of material on a daily basis; fifty pages of dialogue was the norm. To put that in perspective, on a film you might shoot two pages in a day. It was trial by fire. I realized the challenge and began getting more and more comfortable doing it, in large part due to Gloria's support. She had an impact on helping me grow as a professional, which is why it would mean so much to me when I had the chance to have a significant impact on her career.

Gloria comes from a musical family. Her mother sang professionally, and her father played trumpet for the Tommy Dorsey Band. Long before she'd established herself as a TV star, she was a successful singer and songwriter. Gloria is one of the few artists to perform two nominated songs on the Academy Awards show. And, with Alan, she cowrote the theme songs for the hit TV shows *Diff'rent Strokes* and *The Facts of Life*. Singing was Gloria's first artistic love, although she had little time to embrace it. Between driving her two sons to school and soccer practice, and the grueling shooting schedule of an hour-long daytime soap, she had to work overtime to perform or record in the studio. How busy was she? Well, the vanity plates on her 450 SL Mercedes (a car she had for about fifteen years and kept repainting to make it look new) read: "WHERES G" because she was always on the go.

Then one day, Beth Milstein, an associate producer on *Days*, came across a demo of a song that was sent into the show called "Friends and Lovers." She turned Gloria on to it. The demo was a duet with a male and female voice. Gloria was friendly with Al Jarreau and thought about asking him to sing the other part, but that's when fate would intervene.

My agent invited me to go with him to a club on Wilshire Boulevard in Santa Monica called At My Place to see Carl Anderson perform. Carl had an incredibly diverse career as an actor represented by my agent, as a singer for the Motown label, and on Broadway in *Jesus Christ Superstar*. As I watched and listened to him perform that night, I was blown away and immediately knew that Gloria had to record "Friends and Lovers" with Carl. I believed if she did it would be a hit. I went home that night with a cassette of Carl's latest album in hand and conveyed the same to Gloria. She had recently been lamenting that she was never going to have a hit song. Well, that was about to change in a big way.

Gloria and Carl first performed "Friends and Lovers" on *Days of Our Lives* in 1985. Released in 1986, it shot straight to number one on the pop charts and remains a standard love duet today. Due to the success of the song, Gloria began headlining in Las Vegas and Atlantic City. She appeared and performed on the most popular talk shows of the day and was booked to sing at private events all over the country. She couldn't have been happier professionally, or personally. On top of that, our relationship kept growing. We loved and supported each other. Gloria felt safe with me and appreciated that I lifted her up, which were both new experiences for her. Difficult to believe that anybody would treat somebody that kind, bright, beautiful, and talented in a way that was less than respectful and supportive. But that had been the case. Around a year into our relationship, Gloria wrote and published a book on juvenile diabetes. Her son Brennan had been diagnosed with the disease at four years old, and Gloria became his champion and a champion for fundraising, education, and awareness of the disease. She dedicated the book to me. It read, "To Donald, who every day in a hundred small ways shows me what love is." Needless to say, I was incredibly touched.

Other than my acrimonious relationship with my executive producer, I was enjoying my experience on *Days*. I was growing as an actor and liked the people with whom I was working. I also loved playing on the *Days* softball team. We were in the Entertainment League and had some good actor/athletes on the team. We took those games very seriously. While being on a soundstage was a new experience for me, being on a baseball/softball field was right in my wheelhouse. Having said that, being a valuable contributor to the *Days* softball team wasn't going to do anything for my job security. It was becoming very clear to me that no matter how professionally I conducted myself and regardless of what improvements I made as an actor, nothing was going to be good enough for Al. That first meeting with him, when he was justifiably put off that I brought up publicity, and the ensuing dressing down he gave me my first day on the set, put us on a footing that never steadied. My relationship with Gloria certainly didn't help matters. There was one occasion when Al called me up to his office and accused me of having leaked a story line. I hadn't, and made it clear to him that I didn't appreciate being called on the carpet for something I didn't do. I asked him to tell me who made the claim and told him to get whoever it was on the phone while I was in the room. He refused. I said he had better double-check with his source. About an hour later, I was called back to his office, and he said the reporter had given him my name by mistake. He then said, "Well, that's one thing out of the way." No apology. If I had any doubt, I knew right then and there that my time on *Days* would be short-lived.

Nine months from the day I started on the soap, I was voted Best Newcomer by *Daytime TV* magazine, which at that time was the bible of the industry. YAY! That same week I was fired. Classic!

On top of being killed off, the episode where they pulled a sheet over my dead body aired on my twenty-second birthday!

How's that for timing?! My mom DID NOT like that. She also didn't like that I lost my job. Neither did my dad. But come on. You gotta love show business. Let me recap my career to this point: On my first job as an actor, I was the young lead in a film and told by the director on the first day of shooting that I was going to be a star. Two weeks later, the film was shut down. On my next job, I was voted the best newcomer and fired in the same week! Still, I wasn't disappointed. And I wasn't concerned. I would keep trying, and something good would happen. I told my parents that I would have another series within four months. I don't know why I picked that number, but I did.

And, besides, I took some excellent things away from my experience on *Days*. I was glad to leave, given the oppressive nature of my relationship with Al, but I also learned a lot from the situation. I knew that that experience would serve me well moving forward. Then, of course, there was my relationship with Gloria, nine months under my belt in front of the camera, and a consistent income. My salary allowed me to pay my bills, contribute to my parents' financial well-being, and put money away. Last but not least, there was the celebrity that I gained from the time I spent on the show—and the perks that came with it. I was invited to participate in several celebrity ski tournaments. The timing of my firing was perfect because I was able to attend many of them. They took place at beautiful resorts, and they were all expenses paid. Pretty fun for anyone, but especially for someone who just turned twenty-two.

Now, it's not like I started to get sucked into the celebrity vortex. That type of recognition had no effect on me. I grew up in Los Angeles and around celebrity. My best friend growing up, who also was the officiant at Cindy's and my wedding, was Dick Clark's son Duane. Dick, of course, is an American cultural icon, as the host and executive producer of *American Bandstand* and *Dick Clark's New Year's Rockin' Eve*, among other accomplishments. Duane and I would go to tapings all the time. We would dance on camera and interact with the biggest artists of the day. The Jackson 5, Al Green, The Spinners, Olivia Newton-John, Barry Manilow, and on and on. Duane's dad couldn't go anywhere without a tremendous amount of fan adulation. When some of that began happening to me, it seemed pretty ordinary. In fact, I expected it.

I had an innate belief in myself. I intrinsically believed that I was meant to be in show business and would be successful. Having said that, when you book what you think is a great role in a film and it suddenly disappears, and then book a series and get fired in short order, it tests your resiliency. You have to know that it's not the challenge that defines you as a man, but your response to that challenge. I've said those very words to my sons on more than one occasion.

What I didn't know was, 1984 would test me in ways that I never expected.

CHAPTER 5

Deep End of the Pool Boy

I think people like to exert as much control over their lives as possible. Nobody likes to feel like they're just out there blowing in the wind. A lot of us try to choreograph our world. Nothing wrong with that. Having a blueprint, a map that you believe will lead you from point A to point B, is a good thing. Take the positive steps necessary to get you where you want to go. But—and this was one of my mom's favorite sayings—"Man plans, and God laughs." I've said the same to my kids. Life is going to throw curveballs. Sometimes nasty ones. I've emphasized to my boys that what matters is how you handle them. That's the difference between being a boy and a man.

As I mentioned previously, my final appearance on *Days of Our Lives* landed on my twenty-second birthday—December 31, 1984. Carlo Forenza was as dead as a doornail. I'm not sure if I went out with a bang or a whimper, but either way, I was out. But

I was also smarter. I realized I had to take this acting thing more seriously if I was going to be successful. I had begun to do that before the demise of Carlo. I had started spending time breaking down scenes with a director on *Days* by the name of Steve Wyman. I liked Steve personally and professionally. He knew his stuff, and it was beneficial working with him. In addition to working one-on-one with Steve, I also went back to Nina's class with a determination to hone my craft. As I said, I'm a competitive person, and I wanted to be prepared when my next opportunity came. Despite being fired from *Days*, I'd been pretty lucky up until then. But, as I tell my boys, you need to go with the adage "Luck is preparation meeting opportunity." I didn't want my luck to run out, so I knew I had to start preparing.

Guess what happened? Opportunity came a-knocking. Now, remember, I had told my parents that I would have another series within four months of getting killed off on *Days*. I'd gone through Pilot Season and came very close to booking a job a few times, but hadn't landed one. But Cinderfella was about to find his slipper.

By the mid-1980s, *The Young and the Restless* was one of the most popular daytime TV shows in history. The 1973 love child of Lee Phillips and Bill Bell Sr., *Y&R* was revolutionary in its style and storytelling. It implemented innovative lighting techniques, background music, and camera angles. It also featured a raft of good-looking young actors in various stages of undress. Yes, *General Hospital* might have had a bigger audience, and

Ryan's Hope might have pleased the critics more, but no daytime drama was hipper than *The Young and the Restless.*

Tom Langan, a producer on *Y&R*, called my agent and told him that Bill Bell had seen me on *Days of Our Lives* and wanted me to screen-test for a new character he had created named Brad Carlton. The role was a charming, hardworking, opportunistic kid from the wrong side of the tracks, but one with an innate acumen for business. The Abbotts, a powerful cosmetics dynasty and one of the core families of the show, were hiring Brad Carlton as a groundskeeper/pool boy.

I was vacationing with Gloria in Hawaii when I received a call from Sid informing me about the screen test. Needless to say, I was excited. The scene was faxed to me, and I immediately began working on the material.

On the day of the screen test, I arrived at CBS Television City to find seven other guys testing as well. They had all of us in a room, and the actors were socializing. Not me. I had my game face on and was all business. I had no interest in making friends. I was focused and ready to roll. I didn't approach it any differently than I would an athletic competition. I was called out to the set to receive my blocking and was introduced to Ed Scott. Ed was a producer and director on *Y&R*, and he was directing my screen test. Ed appreciated that a screen test is a high-pressure situation and joked around to put me at ease. When he did, I joked right back. We bonded immediately and have ended up working together for the majority of the thirty-two years since then. He has been a dear friend, a mentor, and today is my supervising producer on *The Bold and the Beautiful*. The day of the test, Ed warned me that the actress I would be working opposite was, and he chose his words carefully, an "eccentric personality." He told me, "Be ready for anything." Her name was Brenda Dickson. She played the trouble-stirring siren Jill Abbott on the show. She lived up to Ed's billing. She was smoking a cigarette during the scene and blew the smoke in my face more than once. I just went with it, stayed present, and gave the performance I wanted to give. When I finished the scene, I knew I had the job. I just knew it, and I was right. *Y&R* cast me as Brad Carlton!

I've probably counseled each one of my sons at various times in their lives that getting a job is one thing. Keeping it is something else. Work to the best of your ability. If you don't know something, ask. Play to your strengths, and if you have a weakness, work harder on it. You'd be surprised, I tell them. You can turn a weakness into one of your biggest strengths. I also suggest that they make themselves indispensable. Control what you can control, and the rest will take care of itself.

I didn't pull those words of counsel out of my butt. I lived them. The *Y&R* opportunity is the first time that I remember being aware of the things I just described. I didn't waste any time patting myself on the back. No jumping up and down. No big celebrations. I was focused on the task at hand: cementing Brad Carlton's place on the show. My first day in the studio, I met the coexecutive producer, the late Wes Kenny. He had a wealth of experience, an extensive résumé both inside and outside of daytime dramas as a producer and director. Wes had a real presence about him, and when he introduced himself to me, he gave me a firm handshake, looked me right in the eye, and was warm and supportive. He went out of his way to make me feel at ease. That was a new experience for me. I would come to find out that actors loved Wes. He understood what we go through, and would go out of his way to get the best performance out of us that he could. As time went on, I would go in the booth during other actors' scenes and watch Wes as he watched the actors on the monitor. At times, it was as though he were playing the scene himself. He would be emotionally invested.

Wes was the best. A man's man, with a great sense of humor, a wealth of knowledge, and totally secure in his own skin. It happened that he was a passionate tennis player. We had fun playing together on a few occasions. Wes moved on a year into my being on the show, and Ed Scott, who trained under Wes, took over. I was truly blessed to have Wes guiding me my first year on the show. I learned a great deal about acting under his tutelage. He was a generous guy, and his largess impacted me from day one.

My first scenes, on my first day, had my character showing up at the Abbott estate having answered their help-wanted ad for a groundskeeper. Of course, I was prepared. I worked with Brenda and felt the scenes went well. I was in my dressing room getting ready to leave when there was a knock on my door. It was Wes. He walked into my room and said, "Good job today. We have work to do, but you've got talent, and if you apply yourself you'll be around here for a long time." I told him that I was going to work hard and that I appreciated his kind words, and him making an effort to come to my dressing room. He walked out, and I was dumbfounded. It was so contrary to my experience on *Days*.

Still, I wasn't about to take anything for granted. I knew that in spite of the supportive atmosphere, an actor's tenure could be short-lived when starting out as the new resident hunk on a soap. As my acting coach Nina Foch counseled me the first time we met, "Your looks are going to be your biggest asset and your biggest curse." And now here I was spending my first few months on the show wearing cutoff Levi's shorts called Daisy Dukes and not much else. I was going to have to prove that I could do more than flex my abs and wield a nasty pool skimmer.

I did. I was fortunate to be put in a story line with a very generous and talented actress, Beth Maitland, whom I love to this day. Beth played Tracy Abbott, the ne'er-do-well daughter of the Abbott cosmetics dynasty who battled self-esteem and weight issues. Beth raised my game. I certainly grew as an actor working opposite her. I was entrusted with some very challenging story lines and relished the opportunity. My character went from the resident hunk pool boy, shirtless the vast majority of the time, to a corporate executive in a three-piece suit.

Things were also going well off the set. I was euphoric in my relationship with Gloria. She was sophisticated, beautiful, and had a great sense of humor, all the things that attract me most about a woman. That she was sixteen years older than I wasn't an issue at all. But our May/December relationship drew more than its share of attention in the celebrity press. The *Globe*, the *National Inquirer*, *People* magazine, and others all ran with it. *People's* story was written like a soap opera script, love-conquers-all style. By today's social media standards, the story definitely would have been TRENDING, but the attention didn't faze Gloria or me in the least.

At home, my parents were supportive of the relationship. If they had any misgivings, they kept them to themselves. I think they were happy that I wasn't wrapped up in the Ilene drama anymore. On top of that, they loved Gloria, and she loved them. She appreciated my dad's sense of humor and generous spirit, and my mom's no-nonsense, what-you-see-is-what-you-get personality. Most of all, Gloria loved the way I loved my parents. She said she found it "eye-opening and heartwarming."

After we'd been dating for about a year or so, we moved in together. At twenty-two, I would have my first foray in parenting boys. Gloria's sons, Brennan and Robin, were around eight and ten years old at the time. They were going back and forth between their dad's and mom's houses. Later, I would have my own experience with divorce and split households, and the experience I gained with Gloria's kids was immensely helpful. A divorce is not easy for any child. I jumped right into Brennan's and Robin's lives. It felt natural to me. After all, I did have a great role model: my dad. Of course, Gloria and I talked about it, and I certainly had the awareness that this was a new situation for her sons and anticipated a period of adjustment. Initially, I just did the things with them that I liked doing with my dad. We would wrestle, play basketball, and throw the football around. We hung out, and got to know each other. That was all great, but it became clear pretty quickly that they were in desperate need of discipline.

It's not unusual for divorced or divorcing parents to let their kids get away with things. Typically, this leniency stems from guilt. The lack of discipline in Gloria's house also came from her self-esteem issues. (I'm not telling you anything she wouldn't.) On the one hand, Gloria's battle with self-esteem baffled me. She was one of the most talented, beautiful, and intelligent people I'd ever met. On the other hand, I also knew that the men in her life had bombarded her with negativity. The constant barrage of hurtful remarks had been so prevalent that she began to believe the garbage being thrown at her.

So not only did Gloria feel guilty about putting her sons through the wringer of her divorce, but she lacked the confidence to offer them the structure they needed.

And they took advantage.

I grew up in a household where parental respect was a must. I don't mean that my home was rigid. It wasn't at all. But something like talking back to my mother was out of the question. I was the baby of the family and could do virtually no wrong in her eyes. It became a running joke. As soon as Dad started getting on me about something, my mom would immediately come to my defense. Dad would then say, "Oh, sorry, I forgot I was talking to The Second Coming!" Having said that, there were certain things from a behavioral/respect standpoint that were clear and expected. As I've mentioned, day to day my mom, who was nurturing, loving, and TOUGH, was the disciplinarian. My dad was my buddy, my playmate. However, if it was something of real significance, my dad brought down the hammer. And if I raised my voice to my mom, which I rarely did, it was as if my dad had supersonic hearing. No matter where he was in the house, I would hear his voice as if it were coming over a loudspeaker: "That's your mother you're talking to!" It simply wasn't allowed, so when I first experienced Gloria's sons talking back to her, I responded just like my dad would have with me: "That's your mother you're talking to."

While there was a relatively brief period where they tested me, a kind of "Who's this guy think he is, telling us what to do?" attitude, they found out pretty quickly that I meant business. Of course, a necessary part of that was Gloria being on board, and she was. She appreciated having a male in the house who drew a line in the sand between what behavior was acceptable and what behavior wasn't. I knew from my experience that actions have consequences, and I impressed the same on Robin and Brennan. For example, the punishment for talking back to their mother would be to write standards like "I will respect my mother's wishes," or "I won't raise my voice to my mother." I'd make them write it 250 times. If they balked, I would double it to 500. If they balked again, it was 750, and so on. You get the picture, and so did they. Other disrespectful behavior might get them grounded or have something meaningful to them taken away. The discipline, none of which was unreasonable, and the structure I insisted on, really had a positive impact on them and their relationship with their mom.

Now, it wasn't as if I was the enforcer at all times. We continued to have a lot of fun together. I enjoyed hanging out with them. What I didn't fully realize at the time was that my being so present in their world was something they needed. Their dad was caught up in the trappings of his elevated celebrity from the success of the situation comedy *Growing Pains,* on which he played the role of psychiatrist Jason Seaver. I don't want to give the impression that Alan wasn't a loving and devoted father. He was, and his sons reciprocated with the same love and devotion. During the time I was living with Gloria, however, Alan wasn't giving his sons the attention or, at times, the example they needed. They were spending a disproportionate amount of time with Gloria and me, and as a result, though I was just in my early twenties, I ended up being more of a father figure than I had anticipated.

It wasn't until thirty years after Gloria and I ended our relationship that I became aware of how much of an impact on Brennan and Robin's life I had. At least on Robin's.

It was the fall of 2015, and I was at my son Luca's football practice when I received a call from my friend Tom Lemming. Tom is a highly respected high school football analyst and the host of *The Lemming Report* on the CBS Sports Network. He spends a tremendous amount of time in his car driving across the country visiting high school football programs. So he listens to the radio A LOT, and on this particular day he was on the road and listening to *The Howard Stern Show*. Robin Thicke was the guest. I don't know how they got on the subject, but Howard ended up asking Robin about my relationship with his mom.

Tom told me that Robin responded by saying that my presence in his life at that time meant a lot to him and he was sad when Gloria and I broke up. He was hoping that we would get married. It meant a lot to him that I treated his mother well and that she was happy. He mentioned that I had gotten him into playing sports and he had enjoyed that.

Tom wasn't my only friend who heard the show. I got calls from a couple of others who told me the same thing. You could have knocked me over with a feather. I had only been in his life for a few years, and all this time later he was talking on national radio about how positive that experience was. I was touched.

It also reinforced in me something that I already knew. Being an ever-present father for your sons is a big deal. All the things that it encompasses—being a friend, mentor, a disciplinarian, and ultimately a role model—matter. I called Gloria to ask her if she was aware of the interview or the depth of Robin's feelings about me at that time in his life. She wasn't aware of the interview but said that Robin having those feelings for me didn't surprise her at all.

But they were still a little surprising to me. Any doubt I still had about Robin's feelings for me would be erased a few months later. In the second week in January 2016, Cindy and I took Alexander and his girlfriend out for a special dinner at Nobu in Malibu. He was returning to school at Indiana University a few days later. Alexander and his date were hanging out in an outside sitting area, while Cindy and I were inside sitting at the bar by the window overlooking the ocean. All of a sudden, Alexander hurriedly walked right by the window and rushed over to us. "Robin Thicke is walking in right now." He knew about our history, and what Robin had said about me on *The Howard Stern Show*. I had been hoping that I would bump into Robin at some point. This was another example, of many in my life, where I put something out in the universe, and the universe delivered.

Even though I didn't know what to expect, I immediately got up, walked over to Robin, put my arm around him from the side, and said, "Do you remember me?"

He turned and looked at me. "Oh my God, Donald," he said, as he threw his arms around me and gave me a huge hug. He then introduced me to his fiancée. "This is Donald. This is the guy I've told you about!"

I introduced them to Cindy, Alexander, and his girlfriend. Robin couldn't have been more warm and gracious. He wanted us to go to the bar and catch up. I don't like alcohol, and rarely drink, but on this special occasion, I downed a shot with him. After the toast, he looked at Alexander and said, "Do you know how lucky you are to have this guy as your dad? He's a great man." I was flattered, and quite moved. He launched into regaling Alexander and Cindy with stories. One in particular made a big impression on Alexander and Cindy, and it was one I had no recollection of. I had taken Robin for ice cream at Baskin-Robbins in Sherman Oaks. We went there frequently. In fact, I grew up going there with my dad. On this particular occasion, we were standing outside eating our ice cream when a woman began screaming that her purse had been stolen. At this point in telling the story, Robin struck a hurdler's pose for dramatic effect. "Your dad sees the guy running through the parking lot, drops his ice cream, and takes off like Superman. He tackles the guy and puts him in a chokehold and hangs on to him until the police came. I'm looking at this guy that I already thought was cool and I'm thinking he is a superhero."

Though we all got a big charge out of the tale, the most poignant thing he said was about how much it meant to him seeing me treat his mother so well. He said, "She really needed that, and it had a very big impact on me." Boys aren't typically very effusive with their feelings, and that wasn't something that Robin had expressed at the time. I realized that I might have missed an opportunity. I know now how important it is to check in with my boys. They might not naturally be open with their feelings, but with a little effort, you can usually coax it out of them. Over the years I've found that to be the case.

It warmed my heart to catch up with Robin. I enjoyed hearing him talk about his own son, and how much he means to him. It was also fun hearing about everything else that was going on in his very successful life. I told him how happy I was for him, and that I was glad we had a chance to reunite these many years later. After we parted ways that evening, Alexander expressed how cool it was to hear Robin talk about me, his dad, as a father figure long before Alexander or his brothers came along. It also blew Alexander's mind that all of this went on in my life when I was the same age that he was.

So back to the story. In 1986 everything was just about perfect. Now I was twenty-three years old, in a great relationship, and a star on the number-one soap opera. I was consistently doing very lucrative autograph appearances all over the country, often traveling with my brother Jack. We would go to shopping malls, Kmart, Sears, car shows, and women's trade shows. Soap operas were at the height of their popularity, and these various venues and retail chains wanted soap stars to attract customers. And it wasn't unusual at all for five thousand people or more to show up at one of these appearances. Between my salary from the show and these ancillary opportunities, I was making a nice living and was very happy that I was able to continue helping my mom and dad.

Bulletproof. That's how I felt. Things couldn't have been going better. My life was firing on all cylinders. But life has a way of making sure you don't take things for granted, and I was about to learn that lesson in a way that I could never have imagined.

CHAPTER **6**

||||||||||||||||||||||||||||||||||||||||||||||||||||||||||||||||||||||||||||||||||||||||||||||||||||||||||||||||

De-bala and Dad

Whatever situations I "perceived" as challenges up to this point in my young life I was able to cope with and persevere. I was happy to be able to share and enjoy my success with my family and friends. It was especially gratifying to share it with my parents. They had given me so much, not the least of which was a belief that I could accomplish whatever I set my mind to. They were always there for me growing up and supported me and participated in whatever I was doing.

It was no different on a fall day in November 1986 when my parents, along with my brother Jack, joined Gloria, Brennan, Robin, and me for a charity walkathon to raise money and awareness for the Juvenile Diabetes Foundation, of which Gloria was the national spokesperson. As I mentioned previously, Brennan was diagnosed with the disease when he was a small child. I remember the walk like it was yesterday, striding along and flanked by my best friends. My dad, wearing his "Best Dad in the World" sweatshirt that I had gotten him for Father's Day, on one side and my brother on the other.

My dad was having some trouble keeping up. He mentioned that his back was hurting. By this point in his life, my dad had stopped working out. It was a far cry from when I was a kid and he had bought us matching navy sweat suits with white zippers. Back then, he would wake me up early in the morning so we could do laps around the house. Even though those mornings were dark and cold, I loved every minute of it! But this was many years later and he was overweight, so it wasn't surprising that the physical activity of a long walk would put some strain on his back. It seemed perfectly normal, but as it turned out, his fatigue wasn't normal at all.

Not long after the fundraising walk, Dad came to watch me play in a celebrity softball game. As it happened, we were one player short and I asked him if he would fill in. He was more than willing. My father had been a graceful all-around athlete when he was younger. When I was in grammar school we would have field day, which included father-son competitions in different athletic activities. Some of my friends would cringe with embarrassment at the athletic inabilities of their dads. Not me. Whatever the sport or activity, my dad delivered. And, on the softball field that day, it would be no different. He loved baseball and had excelled at it in his youth.

He was playing right field and I was at shortstop. A blooper was hit his way. As he attempted to run in for the ball, I could see from his gait that he was struggling. It took everything he had to get there, but he was determined. He ambled his way into short right and made an elegant basket catch for the third out of the inning. After I was done whooping it up and hollering with excitement and pride, I asked him if he was okay. He told me his back was still giving him problems, but he wanted to continue. I'm glad he did, because what happened next was a very special moment for me.

You couldn't script it better. Tie game. Bottom of the ninth. I hit a triple, so now I'm the winning run standing at third base. Two outs. Now who comes hobbling up to the plate? That's right. My dad. The crowd is going nuts and I'm yelling, "You've got this, Dad! You've got it! Rip it!!" The first pitch comes and he intentionally inside-outs the ball, slapping it to right field for a hit and driving me home with the winning run!

We were hugging and kissing, and the joy we felt at that moment over that silly softball game was incredible. Seeing that smile on his face was beautiful. It's a memory that I will never forget, maybe because of what was soon to follow.

It turned out that my dad had been in more pain than he was willing to let on. He had an aversion to doctors and hospitals, so he avoided addressing how he was feeling until he started finding blood in the stool. That scared him enough to let us know what was going on, and to get him to a doctor. Soon afterward we were in an oncologist's office with a doctor telling us that my dad had kidney cancer that had metastasized to the bones in his back. What the doctor said next floored me. "You have about six months to live." Six months?! Wait. No. That can't be! It simply didn't compute. I couldn't reconcile the idea of losing him. He couldn't be dying. In six months? That was not part of the plan. I'd envisioned my life rolling out in a very predictable pattern. I would eventually get married and have children, and my loving father would be there to share in all of it just like he had been by my side for everything else.

My dad said he wasn't afraid of dying, but he didn't want to suffer. Chemo treatments were out of the question. It wouldn't have extended his life significantly, and would have made him very sick. While I selfishly wanted him around as long as possible, I didn't blame him for not stretching out what was inevitable, and I certainly didn't want to see him suffer. The doctors told him that treating the cancer that had spread to the bones in his back with radiation would make him more comfortable, so he agreed to that.

Early in December my dad had surgery to remove his kidney, which had a malignancy the size of a grapefruit. Prior to his diagnosis I had bought my parents tickets to the Bolshoi Ballet for their anniversary. The date of his surgery happened to coincide with the date of the performance. My dad's surgery was in the morning, and he insisted my mother go with my sister Bette to the ballet that evening, My mom didn't want to go, but my dad told her that it would make him happy. At his insistence, my mom relented. My brother, my sister Elena, and I stayed at the hospital with my dad.

The radiation treatments began as soon as he was recovered enough from the surgery. Elena, who lived in New York, would fly back and forth to spend time with my dad. My brother and I would switch off taking my dad to his radiation treatments. *Y&R* was very understanding, and would adjust the daily shooting schedule to accommodate me on the days that I would drive my dad to his treatments. I always enjoyed being in my dad's company, but these drives were obviously especially significant given the circumstances of the finality that we were confronted with. Going back and forth to the hospital we would mostly just shoot the bull. Nothing heavy. We talked about sports, politics, whatever. We tried not to dwell on the elephant in the room, or in the car in this case. On one of those drives he brought up the show. I'd been on *Y&R* for a couple of years at this point, and since he was now home all the time he finally had the opportunity to watch me act consistently.

"You know, Deeb"—or maybe he called me De-bala as he sometimes did—"to be honest, when you started out on *Days* I didn't think you were very good," he said. "But you've come so far, and you're doing a great job now."

I can't tell you how much that meant to me. In my mom's eyes everything I did was wonderful. My dad, however, didn't throw praise around unless it was warranted, so for him to acknowledge my work was really significant. He also expressed that it gave him comfort knowing that I was succeeding in a very competitive profession, that his youngest child was making his way in the world. That wasn't lost on me either. And as a father now myself I understand exactly why he felt that way.

There were many bittersweet and even wonderful moments throughout my dad's illness, but a couple that really stand out.

One day, I was at the airport in LA heading out for an autograph appearance when a tall, good-looking African American man approached me. He said he was a big fan of mine, and that he loved *Y&R*. He looked familiar to me, and as I shook his hand I said, "Haven't we played some pickup basketball together?" At the time I was playing pickup basketball games regularly at the Venice boardwalk and at the men's gym at UCLA.

With some amusement, he said, "I don't think so. I'm Byron Scott and I play for the Lakers."

I don't think I could've felt like a bigger schmuck! I said, "Yes. That's exactly who you are. And I'm an idiot."

You have to understand that I was and am a huge Lakers fan, and still watch them all the time. By professional basketball standards, Byron looked small on television. And even though I had gone to games, I had never been face-to-face with him. I was completely thrown by how tall he was in person. We both started cracking up. That was the beginning of a friendship that lasts to this day.

I wasn't the only Lakers fan in my family. My mom and dad

loved Magic Johnson and were avid followers of the "Showtime" Lakers as well. Of course, so did the rest of the entire population of Los Angeles and much of the world. But the rest of the world's population didn't have the opportunity that we were about to have.

I told Byron about the circumstances of my dad's condition, and his love of the Lakers, and he went out of his way to arrange a clearance for my dad, mom, Jack, and me to attend A CLOSED PAT RILEY PLAYOFF PRACTICE!!!

I made sure my folks and Jack were kept in suspense until the last possible minute. In the car, they had no idea where we were going. My dad wasn't feeling well, but when we got there and Byron was outside waiting for us, he lit up. And when I told him what we were doing, he was blown away. So were my mom and Jack, for that matter. Just watching the practice and experiencing the Lakers so close was a big thrill, but the best was yet to come. After practice, Byron introduced us to Magic, James Worthy, and Michael Thompson. They couldn't have been nicer, and we all took pictures together. I was even able to corral Kareem Abdul-Jabbar, who was walking out of the gym and reluctantly stopped for a picture. When I said the best is yet to come, you probably thought I was referring to the meet and greet, and those pictures. I wasn't. Magic agreed to play a seven-point game of one-on-one with me. That was so freaking cool of him, and Dad watched almost in disbelief. Given that Magic was being so generous, I didn't want to embarrass him, so I let him win. Lol!

Afterward, my dad said, "Deeb, what a great afternoon. That was one of the most special experiences of my life!" That was what I had hoped his reaction would be, so it was very emotional and gratifying for me.

On another occasion, my dear friend Lyle Alzado—NFL star, Super Bowl champion, former Los Angeles Raider, and one of the most intimidating defensive ends of all time—came to visit my dad. Lyle had a big heart and a charming personality that belied his reputation on the field. My dad and I had watched Lyle play on many occasions. My dad also really appreciated his charismatic off-the-field nature. He couldn't believe it when Lyle showed up at the house with one of his jerseys in hand, and gave it to him. He spent a lot of time just hanging out, telling hysterical stories. Lyle was a Brooklyn native just like my dad. AJ liked him right from the start.

That was one of my dad's last really good days. Not long after that, he began to quickly deteriorate. He declined to the point that he couldn't walk anymore. My mom, brother, and I took him to see his oncologist. I wheeled my dad into the room and was standing behind his wheelchair. The doctor came into the room, and my dad asked him point-blank, "How long do I have?"

The doctor replied, "Two weeks."

My mom and the doctor went to discuss something in his office. I was still standing behind my dad's wheelchair as the finality of the doctor's words washed over me. Even though

I already knew my dad was very sick, and it wouldn't be long, hearing the doctor say those words eliminated whatever bit of denial I had left. I broke down like I hadn't at any time prior to this point—even when we were given the initial diagnosis. I just started sobbing in a way I never had before in my life. I bent down and put my arms around my dad and rested my head on his right shoulder. Through the crying I was telling him, "I don't want you to go! I don't want you to go! How can I be talking to you now and in two weeks not have you here?"

He reached up with his right arm and started rubbing the back of my head with his hand. "Come on now, Donald," he said. "Death is just a part of life. We all have to die. You have to be a man now. You have to take care of your mother and sisters." He was emotional, but steady.

I, on the other hand, was crying like a baby. "I don't want to be a man. I need my dad." He said, "I know, Deeb, but it's my time."

It was indeed his time. The doctor was precise in his prediction. The man who had once dreamt of being a farmer spent the last two weeks of his life in the bedroom of his home in Sherman Oaks looking out at the purple blooms of the jacaranda tree he had planted as a seedling years before in the patio. Along with family, we had a wonderful six-foot-four Norwegian Buddhist caregiver by the name of Stig who was able to administer hospice care and helped make my dad's passing as comfortable as possible.

During my dad's last days, he was completely uncommunicative, in a comatose state. Just before he got to that point, I said my last words to him. I leaned down and put my cheek against his and said, "I love you, Dad."

Eyes closed, and motionless, he was somehow able to whisper, "I love you too, Deeb."

Throughout my dad's illness, no matter what was taking place, he insisted that I never miss a day of work. He said that whatever is going on in your personal life should never compromise your professionalism. To that end, at no point during his illness did I miss work. Near the very end, my dad was for all intents and purposes gone. We were waiting for him to pass, but of course couldn't predict exactly when it would take place. I was in a heavy story line on *Y&R* and had a very busy shooting schedule. They would put my scenes up first in the morning so I could go in, shoot them, and go back to my mom's. It was no different on May 5, 1987, when I was in my dressing room running lines with Beth Maitland, just before going out to shoot that day's material. All of a sudden, my door opened and my brother walked in. For the briefest of moments I didn't think anything of it, because my brother would often surprise me at work. But this time was different. I saw the look in his eyes, and the pain on his face, and I knew. I was his little brother, and even though we knew dad's passing was imminent, he didn't want to tell me.

"He's gone," is all Jack said.

I just broke down, and so did my brother. We sat together

and cried. Poor Beth was stuck in the room. She cried with us. We calmed down, and my brother said, "Let's get going." I told him that I had to shoot the scenes. He said he had already talked to Ed Scott, my producer, and he said that we would post-tape the scenes.

"Absolutely not," I said. "Dad wouldn't want that."

I immediately called Ed in the booth and told him I would be out to shoot the scenes. He said it wasn't necessary. We would shoot them another day, and not to worry about it. I insisted, telling him the same thing I told my brother. I gathered myself together, went out, and shot the scenes. My dad wouldn't have wanted it any other way.

I worked the morning of my dad's funeral. Production would have adjusted my scenes to shoot on another day, but as a tribute to my dad, I didn't want anything moved. Ed Scott picked me up at home and drove me to Television City. After I finished my scenes, he drove me to the service.

At the funeral, I barely got through my eulogy for my hero. I was so overcome by emotion that my knees buckled. If not for my brother standing next to me, I would've hit the floor.

At a Jewish funeral it's customary that the family throw dirt on the casket of the deceased. It can be thrown by hand or with the use of a shovel, and is a marker for the deceased's departure from the living world. Ceremonially, it's one handful or one shovelful of dirt for each family member or from my experience, close friends. After that, the maintenance people take over and fill the burial plot with all of the remaining excavated dirt. My brother and I wouldn't allow that. We stayed and buried him ourselves. We wanted to honor him in that way.

My dad's passing would be a marker for me as well. At twenty-four, my world as I knew it was rocked. It was truly a loss of innocence. I became painfully aware of how quickly things change, and that life has no guarantees. I really started taking stock of my life, maybe for the first time, but certainly in a way that I hadn't previously.

"Man plans, and God laughs." That's what my mom said. She was prophetic. Given what was hiding around the corner, a little too prophetic.

CHAPTER 7

He Ain't Heavy, He's My Brother

There was a lot of introspection in the days that followed my dad's passing. Although there were many contemplative moments in the months leading up to his death, reality truly set in when he was gone. I had such love for my dad, and he for me. The memories would roll through my mind like vignettes from a movie. I could see him walking through the front door after getting home from work, and immediately rolling up his sleeves and getting on his knees to wrestle with me. Sliding the catcher's mitt onto his hand and squatting down so I could pitch to him. Playing a game of Around the World in the driveway—he won every time using that damn old-school, two-handed set shot to perfection. He would never let me win.

"You have to earn it," he would say.

It was a great lesson, and I applied it to all my sons. When I finally got that first win, it meant a lot to both of us.

I would also remember throwing the football and appreciating the way he could drop it into my hands time and time again as I ran routes. Or sitting me down in his home office when I was heartbroken at fourteen after my first girlfriend broke up with me. "There are many fish in the sea, Deeb," he lovingly said. "Any girl would be lucky to have you."

I could see us in my mind's eye watching Ali fights, and Muhammad's classic interviews with legendary sports journalist and broadcaster Howard Cosell. My dad would get so engrossed watching a fight that he would move around in his chair as though he were in the ring himself. Incredibly, Muhammad Ali and I would later become dear friends. That would have absolutely blown my dad's mind, as it did my family and friends. I could see myself lying in my dad's lap while he drove us home from a late Dodgers game, cheering me on from the stands at my own basketball and baseball games, laughing together till we cried, and giving me a tongue lashing when I needed it. Even today, thirty years after losing him, there are times when I am overcome by his absence. I often find myself admiringly looking at Cindy, and wishing he knew this dynamic woman that I'm lucky enough to call my wife. He would love her. Our boys would've brought him so much joy. He would've enjoyed all of his grandsons and absolutely reveled in their athletic achievements. Drew was a terrific high school basketball player. Lauren's an accomplished snowboarder. Sasha also excels at snowboarding, and plays tennis. Alexander's accomplishments as a quarterback on the high school level at Venice, and on the college level at Indiana University, are many. Luca is proudly following in his brother's QB footsteps and making his own large imprints at Venice. He's already being recruited and receiving offers from Division I universities across the country as a freshman. Anton/"Tank" is killing it as an offensive and defensive lineman on the football field and a center on the basketball court. Davis is also excelling as a basketball player. There's one exciting athletic experience after another with all these guys, but there is one that really sticks out for me, because I grew up watching the Big Ten Football Conference rivalry games and Big Ten champs against the Pac-10 champs in Rose Bowl games with my dad on television.

It was a cold, damp September day in the Midwest. Cindy and I were excitedly and nervously sitting in the stands in Memorial Stadium with 55,000 of our closest friends, when Alexander, who was unexpectedly starting as a 160-pound soaking-wet freshman quarterback for the Indiana Hoosiers in their homecoming game—which, by the way, was being nationally televised on ESPN in their prime-time slot—scored his first Big Ten Conference touchdown against Michigan State! Cindy and I lost our shit! For me personally, it was the culmination of all the years, and the challenges that came with them, that Alexander and I walked hand in hand toward his dream of being a

DI QB. My wife and I were overcome with emotion as we hugged and kissed after watching Alexander dive into the end zone. As we celebrated, I looked at Cindy and emotionally said, "I wish my dad were here to see this."

She held my face in her hands and said, "He is. You carry him in your heart, so he's always here."

That very special experience in Memorial Stadium with Alexander, along with so many more moments with all my other sons, is why I knew my relationship with Gloria twenty-eight years earlier had to come to an end. I wanted children. I always did. That was clear well before my dad passed away. Gloria had her tubes tied after giving birth to Robin. While there was a period of time where some consideration was given to Gloria having surgery to repair her tubes, we both knew that that probably wasn't a good idea. In that way we were at very different places in our lives. Our day-to-day life together was terrific. The age difference was insignificant. But when I really began to contemplate what I wanted my life to look like in five, ten, even twenty years, it was very significant.

Losing my dad really crystalized things for me. In the days following his funeral I largely isolated myself in my office. At twenty-four I was suddenly aware of my own mortality. How fleeting life is. Where am I, and where do I want to be? I knew that I had to move on, and I finally sat down with Gloria and said as much. It was a difficult conversation, but one she knew was coming. It was painful, but we both knew it was just...time.

I wanted a relationship where I could create my own family. A relationship that would lead to children. Hopefully a boy or two. Really what I wanted was an opportunity to recreate what I had just lost. What was really incredible is that Gloria expressed that she wanted that for me as well. She said that I had come into her life at a time when she was in desperate need of respect, and that I provided that for her. Now she was giving me the gift of her understanding and support during a painful but necessary breakup.

I moved out of Gloria's and rented a two-bedroom cottage-style house in the same neighborhood. My sister Bette brought it to my attention. When I looked at the exterior it wasn't really my thing, but when I went inside it had a charming wood-paneled den with a fireplace. The rest of it was fine, but that den is what sold me. My dad, who loved to work with his hands, wood-paneled the den of the house I grew up in. My dad and I watched sports together all the time in that den, so I found comfort in the smaller but similar space of my new home. I bought furniture and moved in. I had framed a picture of my handsome dad in his WWII army uniform, along with his honorable discharge papers, and hung both above the fireplace in the den. I also hung magazine covers, calendar covers, the *Y&R* Emmy certificate, etc., etc., above my desk.

With my new digs locked down, the transition was complete. I was so emotionally impacted by my dad's sudden death that I had a sense of urgency about my own mortality and moving forward into the next phase of my life. I wasn't just going to enter into another relationship. I was going to enter into the next relationship with purpose. Marriage and children. I wanted to recreate what had been taken from me. I lost my dad, so I would become one. Now the quest for the perfect wife.

I found Cindy. Mission accomplished! OK, so it took fourteen years, three relationships, a marriage, and a divorce to get there. I'm a slow learner.

I had to start somewhere, so I started with an adorable, bright, four-foot-eleven blond-haired, blue-eyed, twenty-four-year-old Jewish girl from Toronto named Shari. A girl being Jewish was never significant to me, but as I was looking at my life moving forward, it did take on some importance for reasons I'll explain later. We had a mutual friend who was showing me pictures in a photo album from a trip she had taken to Greece with friends, Shari among them. Gotta love Greece. Quite a few of the pictures were topless, and Shari's pictures stuck out. I got her phone number, called, and that was the beginning of our long-distance relationship. I would fly to Toronto for a few days, and she would come to LA. If we were ever going to really make a go of it, Shari would have to move to Los Angeles, since my career was anchored there. She did...and it was tough for her. Shari still lived at home in her childhood bedroom, and came from a wonderful close-knit family that I loved. She worked at her father's law firm. You get the picture.

She moved to LA, where she had one friend—and me. My

mom wasn't exactly warm and fuzzy toward her, and my sister had a family of her own. My brother, on the other hand, loved Shari, and vice versa, but the bottom line was, Dorothy wasn't in Kansas anymore. I was ready to get married, have children, and create a real life for us, but she wasn't ready for that kind of life change. I understood, but if we weren't moving forward we were just kind of stuck in a quagmire. It was hard on her, and then it became hard on me, which of course took a toll on the relationship. We talked about it and decided the best thing was for her to go home for a few weeks, or longer, and really figure out what she wanted. During that time apart she did figure it out, and was ready to move back to LA and move forward with our relationship. During our time apart, I was on the fence about what I wanted, but I did love her and, given the time and effort that had been invested in the relationship, I wanted to give it another try. Of course, some things in life succeed or fail based on timing. I don't know that we would have made it either way, but given the gravity of what happened the day after she returned, we didn't stand a chance.

It was a weekend early in March 1989 and Shari was coming in on Sunday evening. The previous Friday my brother and I had flown to the Midwest for an autograph appearance that I had. I would do these weekend autograph appearances frequently, and Jack would come with me most of the time. He really got a kick out of seeing a few thousand woman showing up to see his little brother. It could be pretty heady stuff, but I never let it inflate my ego, at least not any more than it already was. Lol! Thanks to my parents and my solid upbringing, my feet were planted firmly on the ground.

It wasn't that many years earlier that I was in the paper for some high school athletic achievements and my dad said, "It's fun to read about yourself in the paper, but good or bad, never believe your own press clippings."

My brother reinforced this early in my daytime success when he told me, "All the ass-kissing is fine, but never take it for granted, and always treat people well."

It was great advice from both of them, and it has stuck with me to this day. I have given the same advice to Alexander and Luca.

I always had a great time hanging out on these personal appearance weekends, and I had no reason to think this one would be any different. I pulled up to my brother's house in the limo and called him from the car to tell him to come out. He didn't answer. I called again, and he didn't answer. That was unusual, because my brother was nothing if not punctual. I got out and went to his front door and started pounding on it and yelling for him. Nothing. It was out of character and I became very concerned. I kicked in his door and there he was in his underwear coming down the stairs.

He looked at me and said, "What the hell are you doing?"

I said, "What are you doing? We have to get to the airport."

He couldn't believe that his alarm hadn't awakened him.

He said he had a bad headache and hadn't slept well during the night and must've finally fallen into a deep sleep. He threw his stuff together and we headed for the airport. That weekend he wasn't quite his outgoing self. He was having headaches and generally not feeling well. In fact, on the flight home Saturday night he asked me to rub his neck and his head quite a bit.

Sunday morning we went to a friend's beach house. Going to the beach together was something my brother and I did on a regular basis. Regardless of the time of year, if it was a nice day, we were there. It was not unusual for me to walk into my dressing room at seven o'clock in the morning and have the phone ring with my brother on the other end.

"Donaldson," he would call me. "What time are you done?" If I was up early in the shooting schedule, we would meet at the beach. My brother owned a ladies' clothing manufacturing company and would do most of his business with clients in New York, so he would finish his day early as well. We would chill for a few hours, spending a lot of time throwing a Frisbee. We'd done this for years, and were very proficient throwing that disk around. This Sunday morning was no different. What was different was that the Frisbee was hitting him right in the hand and my brother was dropping it. He said he was tired, and we shut it down. We spent the rest of the day at the beach, and I went from there to the airport to pick up Shari.

The next day, I was at work and walking out of my dressing room to the set just as my brother walked in. He told me that he had made a doctor's appointment and was going to hang out in my room before heading over to the doctor's office in Beverly Hills. I thought he might've started having migraines, which was a malady that my sister Bette suffered from.

Later that day, I finished my scenes and walked into my dressing room just as my phone started ringing. I picked it up, and it was Shari on the other end. I remember like it was yesterday her saying to me with trepidation and emotion in her voice, "Are you sitting down?" I said cautiously, "Yes. Why?"

She said, "I'm sorry. I don't know how else to say it, but Jack's at Cedars Sinai. He's been diagnosed with a brain tumor."

WHAT?! WHAT?! It's hard to articulate what I felt in that moment. Shock, fear, panic. I grabbed my stuff and bolted out of my room. Cedars was just down the street, minutes away. I'm sure I made it in five. I ran through the hospital to his room and opened the door to find him lying on his side, sobbing. He was in physical and emotional pain. We just looked at each other without saying a word. I lay on the bed next to him, and put my arms around him. We cried together. He had been diagnosed with a malignant brain tumor. A grade 3 astrocytoma. It was inoperable, and terminal.

I was in the hallway about an hour later, after talking to the doctor and finding out that it was unlikely that my brother would make it through the year, when my mom and Bette arrived. They knew Jack had a tumor, but had no idea how grave his condition was. I had to deliver that extraordinarily difficult news. My mom buried her husband May 5, 1987, and less than two years later was confronted with the reality that she would have to do the same for her firstborn son. Devastating. I held my mom and sister as they cried. This was a rarity for my stoic and tough Dutch mother. I had to tell my sister Elena over the phone. Again, brutal. She would get on the first plane out from New York. That night, when I got home, I lay on my bed, curled up in the fetal position, and cried inconsolably. I still wasn't over watching my dad deteriorate and pass away. My brother and I took so much comfort in having each other after we lost Dad. My dad made a point of asking us to take care of Mom. Now this. By no fault of her own, Shari's presence was of no comfort to me, and she would end up moving back to Toronto. I knew that my brother was the only relationship I was going to devote myself to in the coming months.

The night of my brother's fatal diagnosis, I went to sleep broken. I woke up brokenhearted, but resolved. I would make whatever time my brother had left as special as I could for him. I was shaken and emboldened at the same time. I simply wasn't going to wallow in self-pity. I was going to focus on what I could do for my brother. I knew that's what my dad would expect of me, and that's what I was going to expect of myself.

I left for work that morning with that attitude, and with my video camera. I checked in with my brother on my way to the studio, and I was okay on the drive. I was good pulling into the parking lot at CBS, and walking onto the set for blocking.

I was good…until I saw my producer and friend Ed Scott. I thought I was hiding it well, but I guess I wasn't. Ed could see that something was wrong. He asked if something was bothering me, and I fell apart. I started bawling, and told Ed about my brother. He hugged me, and consoled me as best he could. He knew my brother well from his many visits to the set, and was very saddened by the news. He couldn't believe this was happening so soon after my dad had passed. We talked, and I pulled myself together and went about being a professional for the rest of the day, and for the duration of my brother's illness. Again, that's what my dad—and brother, for that matter—would have expected of me, and I was going to deliver. I didn't want anybody at work to feel awkward or uncomfortable in my presence. I made sure to joke and have fun with my castmates and crew during rehearsal as I always did, and when the red light came on, to bring it.

After I wrapped that day, I headed straight for Cedars Sinai which, thankfully, was minutes from the studio. The next morning my brother was scheduled for brain surgery. The neurosurgeon was going to do a biopsy for confirmation of the diagnosis from the imaging, and to drain fluid. Later that evening everyone had left, and it was just my brother and me. As I sat there looking at my handsome brother, I knew it was the last time that I would see him looking that way again. The cancer, steroids, radiation, and chemo would take their toll. I told my brother that I brought my video camera. I asked him if, God forbid, something went wrong during the surgery, did he want to express any feelings or thoughts for family and friends on video. I promised him that nobody would see the tape, including me, until he was gone, be it the next day or in thirty years. He liked the idea, so I put the camera on the tripod, hit record, and walked out of the room.

I sat down on the floor in the hallway and reflected on my relationship with my brother, and the many special times we shared. There were a couple of more recent ones that really stuck out for me. It was important to my brother that we visit our hometown together. We moved from Lido Beach, New York, when I was three years old, but my brother and older sister, Elena, grew up in Lido, spending their formative years there. My brother loved LA, but was a New Yorker through and through. We took that trip a couple of months before he got ill, and it meant the world to both of us that we did. I saw all of his old stomping grounds, including the pool where he set many AAU swimming records, and the boat yard where he worked as a teenager. We also visited the house I lived in for the first three years of my life, and many old family friends.

The last visit was to see my paternal grandmother, Grandma Feinberg. That interaction made an unintended indelible comedic impression that had my brother and me laughing till we cried. Now, she wasn't all that communicative, and she wasn't all there mentally, but there were a few things that she made sure to impress upon me before we left. Maybe she thought my brother was a lost cause, but there was still hope for me. Jack kissed her goodbye, and then I leaned in to do the same, at which time she firmly grabbed my arm, and I mean with a vice grip, and intensely said the following, repeating each phrase three times: "Hold the money! Hold the money! Hold the money! No shiksas [gentile girls] in the night! No shiksas in the night! No shiksas in the night! Stay a Yid [Jew]! Stay a Yid! Stay a Yid!" WOW! A Jewish grandmother's parting words of wisdom! That could've been a scene from a Billy Crystal movie, or an episode of *Seinfeld*. Classic! I've stayed a Jew, so that's one for three on the advice. Definitely not what Grandma Feinberg, may she rest in peace, was hoping for, but a great batting average for a Major League baseball player! Lol! A perfect end to a trip we had talked about making many times, and were both very thankful that we finally did.

The other event to really stick out took place about a year before he got sick. I did the lion and tiger act on the show *Circus of the Stars*. Ringling Brothers and Barnum and Bailey Circus has now folded, due in part to other entertainment competition, and to animal rights groups' efforts to stop the use of and cruelty toward wild animals in circuses. Growing up, however, I was a big fan of Gunther Gable Williams, Ringling Brothers' star wild animal trainer. He was known for his soft-spoken and gentle technique in training wild animals. I was in awe of his performances with the big cats, so when the opportunity presented itself to try out for *Circus of the Stars*, I jumped at the chance in the hopes that I would be selected to do the big cat act.

Back in the day, celebrities would go and audition at stuntman/circus acrobat Bob Yerkes's backyard. We would walk along a tightwire that was just a foot off the ground, and swing on a trapeze. I wasn't interested in either of those. I wanted the big cat act, so on the information sheet I wrote in huge letters, "I WANT THE CATS!" I was bummed when I heard from my agent that they were using a prime-time star for the act; however, that would turn to elation when that star—they wouldn't tell me who it was—backed out. Apparently, he found out that working in a cage with three lions and two tigers wasn't a walk in the Serengeti. Now the producers were in a frantic search to find somebody stupid enough to take on the act. They started combing through the information sheets, and found one idiot who had actually written, "I WANT THE CATS!"

Next thing you know, my brother and I were at Universal Studios for what you might call an audition. In this case my scene partners were lions and tigers. Since the celebrity they originally cast backed out, the producers wanted to make sure that the guy who wanted to do the cat act so badly would actually get in the cage. It blew my brother's mind that fate had intervened, and I was going to work with the big cats. While I was blindly overjoyed, he was excited for me, but also concerned.

The audition, which was really just a test to see if I would step in the cage with the cats, amounted to me standing next to the trainer, putting a piece of meat on the end of a stick, and feeding it to the lions. I'm not sure I can fully articulate how my adrenaline was pumping just doing that. The next day, we were off to the races.

The first thing my trainer, Mike Clark, instilled in me was that "the cats are trained, not tame, so don't ever take anything for granted." He told me that "Peaches, the contact cat, will play with you like she plays with Herman, the 500-pound male, and the only thing they respect is aggression."

My brother was taking all this in, and while he appreciated the balls it took for me to go full steam ahead, he recognized that I really was taking my life in my hands. I didn't even consider that, until one day during rehearsal—and it was a rehearsal where they happened to be shooting footage for the show—there was a point in the act where I approached the lion while she was on her podium, scratched her head a bit, then turned around and pulled her head down next to mine to cuddle. Instead, when I turned around, Peaches grabbed me by the back of my neck with her mouth and brought her right leg under my arm aggressively. It happened in the blink of an eye, and thankfully I reacted as trained, yelled at her, and hit her in the side of the head. She released me. Whether or not she was playing was irrelevant. That could've ended very badly, very quickly. What happened to Roy Horn, of the magician/tiger training team of Siegfried and Roy fame, is a perfect example. Had the internet existed back then, where you can see all sorts of big cat trainer tragedies, I don't know that I would have taken on the act.

Anyway, Phil Braverman, the producer, was yelling to get

me out of the cage, and my brother was moving to charge into the cage. That would not have been good, but I loved that my brother wouldn't have hesitated if it meant coming to my aid. I had everybody cool their jets, and continued rehearsal. I couldn't let Peaches or the other cats sense that I was scared, and actually, in that moment, I wasn't. I was angry. My adrenaline had never pumped like that before, and hasn't since. I aggressively continued with rehearsal, so the cats would know that I was the boss. In theory, anyway. My older brother was there every step of the way watching over me, including the night that we shot the show. He was in orange *Circus of the Stars* coveralls manning the door to the cage. If anything went awry, it was his job to immediately open the door so help could rush in. I just sat there, reminiscing, lost in thought, until I heard my brother call my name, telling me to come in. I did. I opened the door, and found him emotional. I hugged him and told him I loved him, and he did the same.

He was diagnosed in March and passed away in December. I told my family and a couple of friends that he mentioned in the footage about the tape. We all watched it together. Needless to say, it was incredibly emotional. He was so beautifully real. Just himself. He spoke into that camera like he was having an intimate conversation with each person he wanted to address. He was articulate, poignant, funny, and emotional. The first time he cried was when he was speaking to me.

He started by saying, holding his thumb and index finger apart, "Donald, I loved you since you were this big." I cried the first time I watched it, and every time since. I'm crying as I write this. Twenty-eight years later, having this tape means the world to me. When I want to have a visit, I can see him and hear him. Because of the nature of the video and what he expresses on it, it's given my boys a chance to really know their uncle Jack. What that means to me, and to them, is invaluable.

Equally invaluable were the lessons I learned about how fleeting life can be. How precious the time that you have with your family and friends is. Adversity really does make us stronger, and provides an opportunity for personal growth that you wouldn't otherwise have. You have a choice in how to deal with tragedy. Find the gift in it. If you look hard enough, it's there. In the film *Shawshank Redemption*, Tim Robbins's character, Andy Dufresne, is in prison for a murder he didn't commit. He says, in regard to his determination to break out, "Get busy living, or get busy dying."

My mom used to say, "Life is for the living." I was determined to make whatever time my brother had left as special as I could and to try to be thankful for the time we had had together, and for however much time we had left. In the midst of this very painful and challenging time, I was given a gift of friendship. His name is Ed Skelly. We had known each other since high school through mutual friends, but we were only acquaintances at that point. At the time of my brother's illness, Ed was living just up the street from my house. At eighteen, Ed lost his dad. He knew I lost my dad, and when he heard about my brother's illness, he was blown away, and reached out to me. He expressed his sympathy, and we commiserated. Having lost his dad not that long before, he really understood what I was going through. We would walk down the street and have dinner, go to a movie, or just hang out. The best part was throwing the football at night under the streetlamps after getting home from my brother's place or the hospital. It was a great distraction, and his company meant a lot to me. Ed is a very bright guy, with a unique personality and a tremendous sense of humor. He made me laugh then, just as he does now. Laughter is important, and there were times during the course of my brother's illness when Ed provided that much-needed outlet. There were also times when I just needed a friend, and he was always there. Over the last thirty years, we've been there for each other through thick and thin. So with the loss of one brother, I gained another. A true gift.

In the months that followed Action's diagnosis, I watched my brother go from an energetic man with an incredible physical presence to a very ill man wearing diapers, incapable of caring for himself in any way. Though he certainly had his moments, overall my brother faced his circumstances with courage, grace, and definitely humor. Before he lost all of his hair, he cropped it, and had me buzz "Action" on the side of his head.

"Bucket list" has become a common phrase. Back then you never heard it, but there were some bucket list experiences that I was determined to make happen for him, and in so doing, it reaffirmed my belief in manifesting. Desire it. Visualize it. Pursue it. Achieve it.

. We had recently changed planes in Washington, DC, for one of my autograph appearances. While flying over DC, my brother had commented on how he had always wanted to do a tour of our nation's capital, but just hadn't prioritized it. Well, after his surgery, I prioritized it for him. After clearing with his doctor that he was allowed to fly, I started putting the trip together. It couldn't have gone better. The Capitol was closed, but after I explained the situation to one of Senator Alan Cranston's congressional staffers, she was kind enough to give us a private tour. My brother got to sit in Senator Cranston's chair. He thought that was pretty cool. We visited the Washington Monument, the Lincoln Memorial, Arlington National Cemetery, and the Tomb of the Unknown Soldier. We went to the FBI headquarters, and even shot all kinds of weapons at their firing range, courtesy of an FBI agent who, you guessed it, happened to be a fan of *The Young and the Restless*. Things just kind of fell into place, making a trip that was special in and of itself even more so.

My brother knew that I had arranged a visit to the White House, but what he didn't know was that this would include meeting President Bush. He had wanted to meet President Reagan, but he had just left office. Unfortunately, something occurred that shortened Bush's availability that day, so our meeting was canceled. We were, however, invited to the White House lawn to watch President Bush leave the White House and board his helicopter, Marine One. My brother couldn't stop telling me how much the trip meant to him, and I told him the same. Having said that, I wasn't quite satisfied. He was supposed to meet the president. That still needed to happen. Bush had just taken office, but, our ROCK STAR president, Ronald Reagan, had just left office, AND was living in Los Angeles. Hmmm.

The day after we got home I called the office of President Reagan. A very nice woman answered the phone, and I proceeded to introduce myself, including that I was on *Y&R*, and described the situation with my brother's terminal illness. She was very nice, and explained to me that they got thousands of these kinds of requests on a consistent basis, and that I would have to write a letter to so-and-so explaining the circumstances...blah, blah, blah. I hung up the phone with the impression that the odds were slim to none that I would get a positive response. Dead in the water...FOR ABOUT FIVE MINUTES. That's how long it took for my phone to ring.

"Hello?"

"Is this Don Diamont?"

"Yes. Who's calling?"

"This is Mark Weinberg, President Reagan's press secretary. How can I help you, Don?"

I was shocked, and I'm sure I stammered my answer. "Mark, how is it you're calling me?" At the time, I played for the Hollywood All Stars. We were a softball team comprised of actors who would play against teams comprised of NFL players. Monies raised by sponsorship and attendance went to charity. In 1988, we were scheduled to play a game against the Washington Redskins in RFK Stadium followed by lunch at the White House. For a reason that I can't recall, at the last minute I couldn't attend, but Mark explained that he had done the White House clearances for the members of the Hollywood All Stars the previous year. He told me that he had just walked by the receptionist's desk and noticed my name and number jotted down on her pad. From having done the clearances, he remembered my name. Hence the call. Unbelievable timing! WOW!

The next day, my brother, my mom, my sister Bette, my niece Alyssa, and my infant nephew Drew, and I were meeting with President Reagan at his offices in Century City. Jack didn't know what was going on. I just told him that I had a very special surprise for him. He didn't know that the security at the elevator was Secret Service. Why would he? They're secret.

He just kept asking, "Come on, Donaldson, what are we doing? Where are we going?" Until the doors of the elevator opened, and right in front of him were glass doors engraved with the presidential seal and the words "Offices of President Ronald Reagan." He was utterly shocked. "Donald. Wait. What?! What's going on?…I'm going to meet President Reagan???! No way. No fucking way!"

"Yes, Action. You're going to meet President Reagan."

"I don't understand. How did you do this? I can't. I'm too nervous!"

I laughed, and said, "Well, you are doing it, so you better get yourself together."

Jack replied, "I can't go first! You go first!"

We were brought into the reception area, and then Mark Weinberg took us into President Reagan's office. We walked through the doors and there he was. He was standing in front of his desk looking every bit like Ronald Reagan. He was tall and handsome with a tremendous presence!

He very warmly said, "Welcome. Please come in."

I approached President Reagan, we shook hands, I handed him a gift of appreciation, which was a silver Tiffany frame (if this wasn't a "what do you get the guy who has everything" situation, I don't know what is), and expressed my gratitude for his willingness to take the time to meet with my brother and my family. Then I introduced my brother, who was bursting at the seams.

He shook hands with President Reagan, and then spontaneously said, "I've got to give you a hug!"

Quick as a cat, he embraced the president. Equally as quickly, two Secret Service agents moved toward President Reagan and my brother in the embrace. Only my brother! I watched this unfold as if in slow motion.

President Reagan motioned to the agents to stay put, telling them it was okay. Then while still in the embrace, he said to my brother, "You're going to beat this thing."

It was an unexpected and emotional moment. Next my mom was introduced to President Reagan. This was no small event for her, either. She'd had a crush on Ronald Reagan since his movie days, so she was absolutely over the moon. The whole family took pictures with President Reagan. Mark had their staff photographer present for the meeting, so we ended up with some wonderful pictures. I was really struck by how warm and engaging Reagan was. I expected, and it would've been enough, to just meet him and take a few pictures, but that wasn't the case. He patiently and sincerely answered all my brother's questions, and showed him some various memorabilia that he had on his shelves. We were there for around half an hour. When we left, my brother was hugging me, and asking me how I pulled it off. He really couldn't believe what he had just experienced. He was truly overjoyed.

A couple of days later, I was back in President Reagan's office. Mark had gotten the photos back, and President Reagan personalized every one of them as I was standing there. I had also asked Mark if it would be okay if I brought some *Time* magazines with the president on the cover, for him to sign. He happily signed those as well, and shared stories with me about the various covers. It was a surreal experience. This was the man who had just left the presidency of the United States, and brought about the collapse of the Soviet empire, and with it an end to the Cold War. I was watching as he stood at the Berlin Wall and uttered the famous demand, "Mr. Gorbachev, tear down this wall!" Now here I was just hanging out, shooting the shit, as he signed pictures for my brother and our family. Very special! I didn't know it at the time, but I had one more trick up my sleeve for my brother, and thankfully, President Reagan was a willing participant.

August was approaching, and my brother's fortieth birthday was on the fifteenth. I was putting together a video for him that included birthday wishes from friends and family. I also wanted to include a few special guests. My brother was a big fan of Rick Dees. Rick is the legendary radio personality, probably best known for the *Rick Dees Weekly Top 40* countdown. He was kind enough to wish my brother a happy birthday on the video by doing one of his popular morning show characters named Willard. Dick Clark joined in as well. I also got the whole cast and crew of *The Young and the Restless* to come out on the balcony at TV City and sing "Happy Birthday" to my brother. The video was great, but then it occurred to me that, just maybe, I could put a cherry on what was already a terrific cake. I called up Mark one last time.

"Hi, Don."

"Hi, Mark."

"How's Jack doing?"

"Well…as a matter fact, his fortieth birthday is rapidly approaching and I'm making this video for him. I know it's asking a lot, but do you think there's any chance…"

I have no doubt that you can fill in the blanks. The next day I was back at President Reagan's office with my video camera in hand.

"Good afternoon, Mr. President. I can't possibly articulate how grateful I am that you would be kind enough to do this video fortieth-birthday wish for my brother."

"Happy to do it, Don. How is he?"

"Fighting the good fight, sir."

"Of course he is. Please give him my best."

"I will, sir. If you're ready, I'll just point to you when I'm recording."

WHAAAAATTTTT!!! To this day, I can't believe it. He went on to do a charming birthday wish to my brother, explaining that a person never turns thirty—they just keep celebrating the anniversary of their twenty-ninth birthday. Then without giving myself time to think it over, I handed the camera to Mark and walked into the shot, extending my hand to the president. As we shook hands, I thanked him, looked into the camera, and said, "Action, happy fortieth birthday!"

Without missing a beat, Reagan followed that with, "Yes. Happy fortieth!"

WOW!!! Cherry, icing, whipped cream, nuts, hot fudge. You name it. It was one hell of a final touch to that video! It meant the absolute world to my brother. He was laughing and crying watching the video, and when we got to the very end and there was the birthday wish from President Reagan, he about fell off the couch. When it was finished, he started hugging me, expressing his love and gratitude. We were both crying, and I told him I loved him too. What a gift!

One could say that the way that all worked out with President Reagan was a matter of luck, fortuitous timing, or happenstance. One could also make the argument that it was somewhat otherworldly. I have to go with otherworldly given the next two experiences that I'm about to describe.

· ||||||||||||||||||||||||||||

Within days of my brother's brain surgery, I started making phone calls with the goal of making some special things happen for him in the short time he had left. The first call was to Lee Rice, the casino executive at Caesars Palace who took care of Action Jackson. My brother and I were going to the Sugar Ray Leonard/Tommy "The Hitman" Hearns rematch on June 12. I told Lee of my brother's diagnosis and prognosis, and asked him if he could please get us ringside for the fight, and into the after-party so that Jack could meet Sugar Ray. He was a superstar at the top of the boxing world at that time, and we were both huge fans, and I knew this would be a huge thrill for my brother. Lee, who really had a great deal of affection for my brother, made it happen.

A few months later, my brother was thankfully well enough to travel, and we were sitting ringside at Caesars Palace among the biggest stars of the day. Jack had no idea we would be ringside, and was on cloud nine. We watched a tremendous twelve-round fight, in which Sugar mounted an incredible comeback, with the fight ending in a draw. That's, of course, a little bit like kissing your sister, but it was a hell of a fight. Off we went to the after-party, but Ray ended up not going. Jack was disappointed, and I was bummed, because I really wanted to make that happen for him. We had watched probably every one of Ray's fights together, and were at Caesars Palace for his fight against Marvelous Marvin Hagler.

About three or four weeks after the fight, my brother had an experimental procedure in which a couple of small holes were drilled in his head. Catheters were inserted through the holes, and radioactive seeds were put through the catheters directly into the tumor. The hope was that the radiation would kill or shrink the tumor. The day after the procedure, I worked into the evening at *Y&R*, and afterward went to my gym, which at the time was called Sports Club LA, to get a quick workout in before going to visit my brother at St. John's Hospital.

In the days and weeks after the fight, I had told many people about the Leonard/Hearns fight experience that I shared with my brother, including Ray not showing up at the after-party. I was telling people that one way or another, I was going to make sure that my brother met Sugar Ray, but to this point my efforts had come up empty.

Back to my quick workout at Sports Club. I had debated even going, because I wanted to get to the hospital to visit my brother. Since it was on the way to St. John's, I decided that I would stop in and get a thirty-minute lift in. I don't know if it ended up even being that long, because I was anxious to see my brother, so I really rushed through it. I finished, hustled down to the locker room, grabbed my stuff, and was heading quickly toward the exit when this black guy passed me going the other direction. He looked very familiar to me. In fact, he looked like Sugar Ray Leonard.

I stopped dead in my tracks, had the briefest of conversations with myself, turned on my heels, and walked up to this gentleman, who I could now see quite clearly was Sugar Ray. I didn't hesitate. I introduced myself, told him what I did for a living, and said that I'd had some unusual requests made of me, and I was about to make an unusual request of him. I proceeded to tell him the whole story about my brother and how we had anticipated meeting him after his fight. I told him that my brother had just had a procedure done and was ten minutes away at St. John's Hospital. Yes, you guessed it: I asked him if he would come with me and visit my brother for a few minutes. The crazy part is, he said YES!

Off we went. When we got to my brother's room, there was the STOP RADIATION sign on the door. Ray didn't flinch. We put on lead suits and opened the door. The lights were out and my brother was sleeping.

I said, "Action, it's Donald. I have somebody with me who wants to visit you. I'm turning on the lights."

We moved to the foot of his bed. He was understandably a little groggy, and he looked at us through squinted eyes. "Donaldson, what are you doing? Who's here?"

I proceeded to ask him a couple of questions. "What's the last trip we took together?"

"Vegas."

"Why did we go to Vegas?"

"To see Sugar Ray."

"Who is standing at the foot of your bed?"

Jack hesitated, then gathered himself, forced his eyes open, looked in disbelief, and said, "What the fuck??? This is impossible! No fucking way!?"

Ray said, "It's me, Jack. I bumped into your brother, and he told me the whole story, and I had to come see you."

My brother sat up, putting his legs over the side of the bed while explaining to Ray and me, "I could make out a black guy standing next to Donald, but I thought you were an orderly." He certainly didn't expect that Sugar Ray Leonard would be standing at the foot of his bed.

Ray cracked up! "No, Jack, I'm definitely not an orderly."

As it happened, my brother was carrying the photos that we took at the fight, which included photos of Ray in the ring. If there was any doubt how big a fan my brother was, they were put to rest when he pulled those out. Ray was incredibly engaging. We spent about half an hour visiting with my brother. Before we left, Ray hugged my brother while wearing his lead gown, and told Jack he had no doubt that he was going to get well and that there would be two ringside seats waiting for him for his fight on December 7. We left, and I drove Ray back to Sports Club. Before we parted I hugged him, and told him that I couldn't possibly express my gratitude. That was truly how I felt. He was one of the biggest stars on the planet. A living legend who jumped in a car with a stranger to go visit his terminally ill brother. It's still hard for me to believe that actually happened.

True to his word, the tickets arrived for his match against Roberto Duran. The battle took place on December 7, 1989. Ray won his fight. My brother did not. He passed away the night before, on December 6.

Was that experience with Sugar Ray Leonard another incredible coincidence, or did I manifest it? Well, three's a charm. If what I describe next doesn't drive it home for you, nothing will.

As I said, within days of my brother's brain surgery, I started making phone calls, bound and determined to accomplish some things that I knew would have special meaning to my brother. In addition to calling Vegas, I started making phone calls in hopes of finding a way for my brother to meet Yankees baseball legend Mickey Mantle. Action grew up worshipping Mickey. When Jack was a little kid, my dad would take him to Yankees games, and he would scream for Mickey Mantle. His love for Mantle never waned, and my brother always spoke of how he would love to meet him. My efforts to make that happen, which went as far as to offer paying a significant appearance fee, came up against a brick wall.

I was frustrated, and still mulling over in my head how to make it happen, when as I was walking out my front door to go to work, my phone rang. I ran back in, answered the phone, and it was my agent at the time, Sid Craig. He was well aware of my efforts to get to Mickey Mantle, so he was incredibly excited to tell me that he had been talking to the talent booker for *The Pat Sajak Show*, and had just found out that Mickey Mantle was going to be a guest on the show that evening. Where did *The Pat Sajak Show* tape, you might ask? At CBS Television City, one floor above the *Y&R* soundstage. Sid had already told Vic, the talent booker, about my brother and me, and told me to call Vic. I did. He was wonderful. He told me what time to have Jack in the green room for the surprise.

I called my brother and told him that I needed him to be dropped off at CBS for something important. No matter how persistent he was in asking me what was going on, I wouldn't give. Later that afternoon, I took Action up to *The Pat Sajak Show* green room, and we sat down on the couch. He kept saying, "What now? What's going on?" Then one of the production assistants walked by, saying Mantle was in the building, on his way up. The jig was up, and my brother turned to me with tears instantly welling up in his eyes, asking, "I'm going to meet Mickey Mantle???"

I said, "Yes, Action. You're going to meet Mickey Mantle."

He was dumbfounded, emotional, and excited as he hugged me and said, "Thank you, Donaldson!"

As we waited for Mickey, I explained how I had been trying to get to him, and how this had unexpectedly finally happened. Then in walked Mickey, who had been briefed on his way up. He was incredible with my brother, and exactly who you hoped he would be. Of course, the first thing he did was ask for a drink. We spent about forty-five minutes with him. We walked out of there—well, I walked, but my brother floated.

As my brother's condition was deteriorating, he would often talk about his experiences with Reagan, Sugar Ray, and Mickey Mantle. It meant so much to me, because it meant so much to him. He would recount these stories to anybody who would listen, always saying how he couldn't believe his brother made these meetings happen. I pinch myself about them even today. I think about the line from the movie *Field of Dreams*: "If you build it, they will come." I put these thoughts and desires out there on my brother's behalf. I went to great efforts to make them happen, and somehow, someway they came together. I can't possibly write it off as sheer luck, or happenstance. As with other events in my life, I saw it in my mind's eye, and took steps to find my way there. You put one foot in front of the other and start walking toward that clear goal. Sometimes it might lead you down another path you didn't anticipate, to a beautiful surprise. And you say to yourself, "Aah, that's why I started down that original road. To get here." I have in different circumstances conveyed this to my boys, at different times in their lives. The same holds true if you want to keep rolling down a negative path. Shit rolls downhill, and that shitball can get bigger and bigger. More about that later.

As Jack's condition worsened, he simply couldn't care for himself in any way. I would shave him, wash him, change his diapers. It's hard for people to hold on to their dignity in those circumstances. I would find ways to joke about it with my brother, and it allowed us to laugh our way through it. Gallows humor, I suppose. Sometimes we cried. It was getting harder for him to communicate, and my sister Elena made me aware that he had conveyed to her that he was feeling guilty about leaving me. He felt that if he stopped fighting, he would be letting me down.

I had no idea he was carrying that burden, and I felt terrible about it. I immediately went to my brother, and told him that I loved him, he didn't need to worry about me, and he didn't need to fight one more minute than he wanted to. Whatever fight he was putting up, to do that for himself, never for me. You see, after my dad passed, Jack and I often talked about how lucky we felt to have each other as the remaining males in the family. He knew that in his absence, all of the patriarchal responsibilities that we shared would be mine. I reassured him that I was up to the task, and as such, would honor him, as we did our dad. With tears in my eyes, I told him that I would carry him in my heart, so he would never really leave me anyway. He looked at me through the tears in his eyes with what I can only describe as profound love and gratitude. I kissed him and hugged him, and again told him that I loved him. He whispered the same to me.

Finally, I told my brother that when he was ready to let go, I would be right there at his side. And I was. We all were. Including

Florence, the grandmotherly private nurse we hired for Jack in the last weeks leading up to his passing. She was right out of central casting. Florence insisted that "Jackie" eat to keep his strength up. He loved her, and loved teasing her. She was constantly trying to get food in my brother's mouth, and he'd tell her, "Climb in this bed with me, and then I'll eat." Even when my brother could no longer speak, and we were nearing the end, she would still try to get him to eat. He would look at me with an eyebrow raised and roll his eyes like, is she kidding? But he would do it, until he no longer could.

He took his last breath in the early evening of December 6. It was a combination of relief and sorrow. We stayed with him through the whole after-death process, including when they placed his body in the bag. At that point, Elena, Bette, Jack's girlfriend Sheila, my mom, and I left his room, and began sadly and exhaustedly walking down the hall heading home. Florence stayed behind. Suddenly, and urgently, I said "Wait!" Everybody asked, "What's wrong?" I answered, "Do you think there's any chance Florence is still going to try and feed him?" Everybody laughed the laugh that breaking tension brings. There was that gallows humor again.

Elena said, "Our brother would've liked that one!"

I think he did. I think he was laughing right along with us.

I don't remember much humor in the days that followed. There was an excruciatingly difficult eulogy, and the burial. I really missed my brother, and my dad. In the span of less than two years I lost them both. The entire male side of my family. The loss was profound. It left a mark. An indelible emotional scar. One that would inform decisions I would make down the road.

‖‖

CHAPTER 8

Fight Club

With Jack gone, I experienced extraordinary loneliness. I wasn't paralyzed in the grief I felt. I didn't lock myself in my house and sit there sobbing. There were moments, though, when something would remind me of Jack and I'd just fall apart. Still, I went about my routine: working, playing basketball at the gym, and going on autograph appearances.

Meanwhile, I was searching for a meaning to a life that I had begun to feel was ultimately unfair. I watched from the sidelines as Jacques and Ilene became embroiled in perhaps the biggest political scandal in France in a hundred years. Jacques was the focus of several investigations into the use of city funds for private purposes. Both he and Ilene were headline news across Europe, and even here in the United States. The novelist Graham Greene, who lived on the Côte d'Azur, published a small book that detailed Jacques's legacy of corruption in Nice. He titled it *J'Accuse* after Emile Zola's famous open missive. The glare of the spotlight got so hot that, in 1990, on a trip to Japan sponsored by the city of Nice, Jacques and Ilene fled to South America.

My relationship with Ilene was like something out of *The Thorn Birds*, a miniseries filled with duplicity, danger, and true love. The true love part was what existed between Ilene and me. The rest of the dramatics were between her and Jacques. She was under enormous pressure both from inside her marriage and outside, and I gladly offered my shoulder for her to cry on. She called me from Uruguay, and we talked on the phone for hours. I did what I could to help her through that extraordinarily difficult period. The fact was, I couldn't rescue her. And the reality was that we would never be together. Always connected, but not as a couple. The realization that I would never be with Ilene wasn't the end of the world. Life goes on. I was still on *Y&R*, single, and living in one of the greatest cities in the world, Los Angeles. Things could have been much, much worse. And, in fact, a series of remarkable events would happen to me during the months and years after Jack's death.

During the 1980s and 1990s, CBS would periodically broadcast a television special called *Night of 100 Stars* to aid the entertainment charity The Actors Fund. One of the stars of the 1990 version of the show was Muhammad Ali. As I already mentioned, my dad, brother, and I were huge fans of Ali's. Turns out, the talent booker for the show called to check my availability. I told my agent even if they didn't book me, just to get me a press pass. I had to meet Ali. Well, they did book me, and not long after, I was off to New York to shoot the show.

When I arrived at the hotel, I went straight to the green room. I saw a guy wearing a Sugar Ray Leonard–Donny Lalonde T-shirt. Close enough, I thought. I asked him if he was there with Ali. His name was Burt Watson, and he was there with Frazier. He looked at me and lit up. Yup. Big *Y&R* fan. On top of that, he happened to be holding *People* magazine's 50 Most Beautiful People in the World issue in his hand. Burt said he just saw my picture in the magazine and asked if I would sign it for his wife. I said, "Sure…as long as you introduce me to Ali." We had a deal! Burt told me he was having dinner with Ali that night and promised to call when they returned to the hotel.

Sure enough, at about twelve thirty in the morning, my phone rang. Burt said, "Hey, we're coming up" and told me what floor to meet them on. I threw on my clothes, pounded on my agent Sid's door, and ran like a bat out of hell up several flights of stairs. Within a minute of my getting there, the elevator door opened, and there was Ali.

I was in awe. Burt introduced me, saying, "This is Don Diamont, Champ. He stars on *The Young and the Restless*." Ali just stood there looking at me for a few moments. I didn't know what to say or do, until came that famous whisper.

He looked at Burt and said, "He's pretty."

I responded, "No, Champ! No! You're the pretty one. Nobody is prettier than you!"

Ali cracked up. We talked for a minute. I showed him my magazines, and asked him if he would sign some of them. Sid had shown up by this point, and Ali invited us to his room. I couldn't believe it, but he signed every magazine, and we just hung out for at least an hour. Sid told him about the *People* magazine and Ali wanted to see it. Sid had a few in his room, and Muhammad insisted that I go get one, so he could show it to his wife Lonnie. I quickly ran and grabbed one, brought it back, and Muhammad went into the bedroom and—hysterically—woke Lonnie up to show it to her. We took pictures together that evening, and spent a lot of time together over the next few days in New York. I took a picture with Ali, Frazier, and legendary broadcaster Howard Cosell. I immediately went to a one-hour photo shop, and had the picture made into an eight-by-ten. They all signed it for me, and it is to this day one of my prized possessions.

When I got home, I sent Muhammad and Lonnie flowers thanking them for being so welcoming and kind to me. I came home from work the day after I sent them, and saw my message light blinking on my answering machine. That's right, people actually used answering machines in the '90s. Lol! There was a message from Muhammad thanking me for the flowers and telling me that he would call me when he was coming to LA so we could hang out. It blew my mind.

What blew my mind even more is that he did in fact call me when he was in LA, and we went to dinner at the Palm. He came to visit the *Y&R* set. Almost nothing could bring production to a standstill, except Muhammad Ali walking onto our soundstage. Everyone, and I mean everyone, was gathered on the stage, and when Ali showed up you could hear a pin drop. I looked at everyone and said, "What's wrong with you guys? He's not going to bite you."

In truth, I understood what they felt, because it really was awe inspiring to be in his presence. As always, he was wonderful with everybody. Laughed, joked, took pictures, and signed autographs for everyone. We spent a lot of time together in the following years, including my visiting the Alis at their home in Berrien Springs, Michigan, being at the Oscars together when the documentary *When We Were Kings*, chronicling the Rumble in the Jungle, won the Oscar, and Muhammad coming to my first wedding. I told virtually no one that he was coming, so the look on all the guests' faces was priceless when all of a sudden Muhammad Ali strolled into the prewedding gathering, and threw his arms around me, giving me a big bear hug. On another occasion, my brother, Ed Skelly, and I hung out with Muhammad in his hotel room. He lay in his bed wearing only his boxers and regaled us with all kinds of stories from his life, including what it was like when he and Elvis hung out together at Graceland. Those stories will stay private, but let me emphasize...ELVIS PRESLEY AND MUHAMMAD ALI hanging out for the weekend at Graceland! Enough said! Those are all special memories, but there are three that really stick out.

The first was when Muhammad and Lonnie came to my house to see Alexander right after he was born. I have wonderful pictures from that evening. There's one photo where it looks like Alexander is looking Ali straight in the face and making little tiny newborn fists! Priceless! Lauren and Sasha each got to put on gloves and go at it with the GOAT! Again, very special pictures!

The second was when Ali came to Sports Club LA to watch me play his best friend—the photographer that chronicled his life—Howard Bingham's son Damon, in a one-on-one basketball game for bragging rights. Damon talked a lot of shit about how he would kick my ass if we played one-on-one. I repeatedly told him he couldn't hang with me on his best day or on my worst. Muhammad had finally heard enough and insisted that we settle it.

They kept the gym open after hours so the Champ wouldn't get bothered. There was definitely some pressure, because there was no way I would live it down if I lost in front of the GOAT. We all shot around for a few minutes, and then it was on! I was probably around thirty-five at the time, fifteen years older than Damon. Muhammad was in my cheering section along with my friend Ed. Damon started with the ball, and hit his first couple of shots, going up early. I told him to enjoy the lead, because once I got the ball, he would never see it again. I was on fire, and proceeded to smoke Damon's ass, to the point that he was lying prone by the time we were finished. Ali grabbed my wrist and pulled my arm up as the victor, and I have the picture to prove it! It was a thrill to have Muhammad Ali holding my arm up in the air and pointing at me as the champ!

I had to save the best for last. One time, Muhammad came into town and wanted to get a workout in, so we met at this boxing gym on a street called Abbot Kinney in Venice. Abbot Kinney is very tony now, with all kinds of trendy shops and restaurants, but back in the day it was anything but. I was going to get in the ring with Ali. To say that I was excited is grossly understating it. We were going to do nothing more than mess around, but it didn't matter. I was going to get in the ring with the one and only, Muhammad Ali! Eileen Davidson, my girlfriend at the time, came along with a video camera in hand. When I was in my corner, looking across at Ali in his, I couldn't even describe the feeling. There was probably a hint of fear. He did know we were just messing around, right??? He knew. And we were. It was incredible how well he could move in the ring, even now with the Parkinson's. We played patty cake for a couple of rounds, and that was it. It was so incredibly special, and I have it on video. I wouldn't be surprised if it's the last video of Ali in the ring.

I've met a lot of exalted figures over the course of my career. Actors, athletes, princes, and presidents, but meeting Muhammad Ali, and our ensuing friendship, stands head and shoulders above all the rest!

CHAPTER 9

Eyes Wide Shut

In 1990, *The Young and the Restless* had overtaken the perennial champ *General Hospital* as the number-one show on daytime TV. My character was firmly entrenched, and I had a huge fan base. *People* magazine had selected me for their 50 Most Beautiful People in the World issue I mentioned earlier, which was very positive publicity-wise. In fact, as a result of being in that edition of *People*, my agent received a call from Grey Advertising in New York, wanting me for their upcoming Fruit of the Loom underwear campaign. That got a lot of press, and was a really nice paycheck, especially for one day's work!

My character on the show, Brad Carlton, had gone from a shirtless pool boy to a power-broker businessman in a three-piece suit. One fan magazine wrote that I was "Daytime's kinder and gentler answer to *American Gigolo*." With hard work, I had grown by leaps and bounds as an actor, which was also due in no small part to the privilege of working with some of the most talented actors in daytime drama. I certainly owe a debt of gratitude to Beth Maitland, Peter Bergman, Jerry Douglas, Melody Thomas Scott, Eric Braeden, Jess Walton, and Eileen Davidson.

I mentioned Eileen was my girlfriend when I got my time in the ring with Ali. Funny how we got there. Eileen, maybe better known today as one of the *Housewives of Beverly Hills*, originated the character of Ashley Abbott and was firmly entrenched on *Y&R* when I started in 1985. She was beautiful and talented. We had sort of a contentious working relationship. It wasn't hostile by any means, but I suppose there was some one-upmanship. Eileen could be a bit aloof, with a biting sense of humor. I was anything but aloof, but had a sarcastic sense of humor. There was some mutual ball breaking back in the mid-1980s. Truth be told, I was somewhat enamored, so maybe I was metaphorically pulling her pigtails.

Eileen left *Y&R* in December of 1988, and I went through my brother's illness not long after, losing him in December 1989. A few weeks after he passed, we had our two-week Christmas hiatus. We came back to work in January, and I was definitely feeling the loss. I was in the makeup chair one January morning, and my friend and makeup man, the late Steve Artmont, was doing my makeup. He was also friends with Eileen, and shared with me that he had been talking to her, and that she was a little hurt that she hadn't heard from any of the actors.

Steve and I shared the same sense of humor, so as soon as he told me that, I said with a shit-eating grin, "We can't have that! I'll call her right now." I jumped out of the makeup chair, walked over to the phone, got her number from Steve, and called her. She answered, and I said, "A little birdie told me that you're feeling a bit blue that you hadn't heard from anyone on the show, so I'm making up for that." We got together for dinner, one thing led to another, and not long after that we were in a relationship, and I was flying back and forth to Vancouver while she filmed a TV series called *Broken Badges*.

We were "in love," and things were moving quickly. Feeling this way was a lot better than feeling the loss of my dad and brother. It was great. I was involved with this smart, beautiful, funny, and talented woman. I was moving forward with my life, on the path to create my own family, have kids, and fix what had just happened. In early summer, we were vacationing in Mexico. One evening we went for a swim in a very romantic, dimly lit private pool area. Unbeknownst to Eileen, I had an engagement ring with me. I waited for the right moment, and then asked her to marry me. Eileen was surprised, and overjoyed, and said, "Yes."

I should've been overjoyed as well, and yet almost from the moment I put the ring on her finger I felt uneasy. Definitely not the feeling you want when you've just gotten engaged. When we got back to the room, Eileen wanted to start calling her mom and sisters, but I was slowing her roll on that. Eileen of course picked up that I was ill at ease, and we talked about it. As much as I wanted to be, I wasn't ready for that level of commitment. In a nutshell, the losses that I'd suffered compromised my judgment. Idealistically, I wanted to marry Eileen, but realistically, I wasn't ready. Eileen was hurt, but incredibly rational, understanding, and emotionally aware. I don't know that too many women would've handled that awkward situation with the grace that she did. Adding insult to injury, she got Montezuma's revenge about a day later. Diarrhea, nausea, cramps, fever, etc. We had a doctor come to the hotel to help her. Turned out to be not quite the vacation we had planned.

Eileen and I were involved for three years, although that third year we were kind of in and out. We were trying to make it work, but it just wasn't. We certainly loved each other, but in some ways, we were a square peg in a round hole.

In 1999, about six years after we broke up, the phone rang in my dressing room, and it was Eileen. We hadn't talked in quite a while, and I was surprised and happy to hear from her. She proceeded to tell me that she was reaching out because she was concerned that I would hear that there was talk of her coming back to *The Young and the Restless*, and she wanted me to hear it from her, instead of through the rumor mill. She told me that *Y&R* had reached out to her, and started giving me all the reasons why she wasn't going to return to the show. I pushed on all of them, told her she was crazy not to come back, and that I would welcome her with open arms. By the end of our conversation, she had changed her mind, and decided she was coming back. Little did we know that our characters, Brad and Ashley, would end up playing husband and wife. So fictionally, at least, we got there!

After Eileen, I made up my mind that I was absolutely not going to jump into another relationship. I had spent the last ten years going from one relationship to the next. I really wanted to try and sort things out in my head and heart. Dating, yes. Relationship, no. I was twenty-nine, and it was going to be the year of the cat. Alley cat! Lol!

One afternoon in 1993, during my period of singleness, I was in my dressing room, having just finished shooting my scenes for that day, when I got a call from *Y&R*'s publicist, Charles Sherman, telling me that Cal Ripken, Hall of Fame shortstop for the Baltimore Orioles, was coming to the studio to visit the set. He said Cal was a huge fan of the show, and of my character, Brad Carlton. He was heading toward breaking a Major League Baseball record that historians said could never be broken: Yankees legend and Hall of Famer Lou Gehrig's consecutive game playing streak. The attention Cal was getting was overwhelming, and Charles proceeded to tell me that when the Orioles were on the road Cal would register under my character's name, "Brad Carlton," so nobody could find his room. I played baseball in high school, and was more than flattered that this living legend had specifically asked if he could meet me.

I told Charles, "Yeah, I think I can hang out until Cal gets here." Are you fucking kidding me???! We became friends, and

Cal invited me to the All-Star Game, which was being held in his home stadium of Camden Yards. I brought my boy Ed Skelly with me. Ed was more excited than I was. He played second base for the Colorado Buffaloes in college and was over the moon at the opportunity to meet Cal and all the rest of the baseball stars that would be at the All-Star Game. The weekend ended up being more over-the-top than Ed and I could ever imagine. The Orioles were playing the Chicago White Sox in the last game before the All-Star break. Cal told us to get to the game early so we could hang out with him and watch batting practice. What we didn't know is that he had a jersey waiting for me with "Diamont" on the back, which I would wear for batting practice. That's right. I was going to take batting practice with the Orioles! SURPRISE!

From the locker room, through the tunnel, to the field I went, in uniform. I started taking cuts with the temperature at 105 degrees with 100 percent humidity. Ask me if I cared. I didn't! It was bad enough that I was taking BP in front of Cal Ripken, but then Hall of Fame legend and Orioles general manager Frank Robinson showed up as well. Second baseman Harold Reynolds was nice enough to give me one of their bats. Well, I got out there and started swinging for the fences. I was hell-bent on knocking one out. But dammit, dreams don't always come true. I hit the warning track three times. Yeah, I know. Almost only counts in horseshoes and hand grenades. Mr. Ripken and Mr. Robinson had a good time giving me shit. I'm still pissed about it today.

I thought I'd had my fun for the day, but Cal had one more trick up his sleeve. He told me I was throwing out the first pitch for their game that day against the White Sox. WHATTT??? Crazy. How cool! Wait a minute. Sold out. Fifty-five thousand people. Hmmm. OK. I got this. Game time came, and I decided, well, if I'm going to do it, I'm going to go out in flames or a blaze of glory. I told Ed that I could just toss it over the plate. I had to bring the heat. Ed said, "Are you crazy? Just toss it." So the announcer introduced me over the PA, and I walked out to the front of the mound. Baltimore was pretty big *The Young and the Restless* country, so I got some decent applause. The Orioles mascot knelt behind the plate, but in my mind's eye I was looking at my dad, just like when I was a kid. Instead of just throwing the ball, I decided I would have some fun with it, and shake my head "no" a couple of times as though I were shaking off signs. That engendered a large round of boos from the crowd. Then I said a prayer, went full windup, and threw the fastball. Prayer answered. Straight over the plate. Boos turned to resounding cheers, and off I walked to high-five Ed and get some props from Cal and the rest of the Orioles. It was redemption for not hitting one out in batting practice. The icing on the cake for that weekend was Cal giving me one of his All-Star Game used bats, which he inscribed with a personal note. It's one of my prized possessions.

Ed and I had a blast that weekend, and two years later, on September 5, 1995, I once again walked onto the field and toward the mound in Camden yards. This time I was participating in the celebration of Cal tying Lou Gehrig's consecutive game playing streak record, which he did that night. We shot a comical skit at Y&R regarding his breaking the record, and they played it on the JumboTron before I was introduced. Michael Minnis, who is *The Bold and the Beautiful*'s cohead writer at present, but was a writer on Y&R at the time, wrote the skit. Melody Thomas Scott, who plays Nikki on the show and was my character's love interest, was nice enough to do it with me. Just as with my Muhammad Ali experiences, I remember standing in the dugout and thinking that my dad and brother wouldn't believe it. After the skit, which played on Cal's "endurance," was shown in the stadium, the crowd went nuts. Onto the field I trotted to congratulate Cal and his wife Kelly on his otherworldly accomplishment. It felt otherworldly to me to be taking part in honoring my friend, the great Cal Ripken!

I think I made it pretty clear that Ed and I had a blast at that All-Star Game weekend in July of 1993. I mean, what could top that??? Hmmm, maybe the trip we took to Honolulu in August, which had nothing to do with baseball, and everything to do with being two single guys in Waikiki. ALOHA!

I really was enjoying my singleness. All was well on the show. I was hanging out with the guys, playing a lot of basketball, and doing a lot of unattached dating—which my kids would refer to as "hooking up." So if you're a single guy, and your personal life's about hooking up, well, what better time to redo your bedroom? Well, that notion that popped into my bachelor head would prove to be a life-altering decision. Would it ever!

Part of redoing my bedroom included new sheets, comforter, pillows, etc. So I walked into this fine bedding/interior design store in Beverly Hills and met a beautiful and engaging woman named Rachel who was working as the in-house interior designer/salesperson. Within a couple of minutes of some flirtatious conversation, this kid comes walking down the stairs of the store pitching a fit. I mean a full-blown tantrum. Turns out this was Rachel's three-year-old son Lauren. As I watched this interaction unfold, it was clear pretty quickly that Rachel didn't have the disciplinary skill set needed to let this child know that this behavior was completely unacceptable. As it happened, Rachel had two sons—the other was an adorable one-year-old named Sasha—and was in an unhappy marriage to a semipresent husband and father who was in financial straits as well.

Rachel and I started to spend some time together. I was able to watch her interact with her boys, and while she wasn't great in the discipline department, she was a good and loving mom. I liked that. She had dark hair and eyes, and while her coloring was completely against type for me, she carried herself with a sophistication that was typical of women that I was attracted to. She spoke five languages, was an amazing cook, and had a great sense of style. I would come to realize later that she had something else as well: a drinking problem.

This is why I talk to my boys about having your eyes wide open when it comes to looking at yourself. Understand your own emotional life and what pushes your buttons. I took Rachel to dinner with several of my friends that she was meeting for the first time. To say she had too much to drink would be an understatement. Suffice it to say that I had to pull my car over on the way home so she could vomit out the door. That was explained away with, "I was nervous meeting your friends, and didn't realize how much I was drinking." Okay. That seemed reasonable. But then there was another incident. That one was also explained away. She assured me there wouldn't be another drinking incident, and for a while there wasn't. But only for a while.

The issue was that I had grown up with a brother who had a problem with addiction, so while I didn't recognize it at the time, elements of Rachel's behavior were emotionally familiar to me. You might say FAMILIAL. Kind of like the child of an alcoholic marrying an alcoholic.

Rachel was open to having more children, which was a must for me, and to converting to Judaism, which at that time in my life was significant. Later in the book I'm going to devote some time as to why that was important to me. For now, however, a whirlwind romance ensued. It was not endorsed by my family and most of my friends. They didn't care for Rachel, but what did they know? A woman with some qualities I was attracted to, AND TWO SONS. Just add water, and...insta-family! That's what was going on in my emotional life, in my subconscious. I recognized that in hindsight, but not at the time.

So what did my family and friends know??? Turns out, a lot! Within a year, Rachel was divorced. We were married. And she was pregnant. After we were married, personality issues that I had seen in fleeting moments prior to getting married revealed themselves in a big way. Belligerence toward people, an irrational temper that fueled reactions to the most benign disagreement. If Rachel felt wronged, no matter how insignificant the perceived slight, her idea of conflict resolution was to gut the perceived offending party like a fish.

There's one experience I will never forget. When Lauren was in grammar school, some moms arranged a carpool. Not surprisingly, there was some miscommunication, and Rachel felt one of the other moms had disrespected her. I knew the mom, and she was a very nice woman. I was confident that something had been blown out of proportion. A "carpool summit" was arranged, and Rachel asked me if I would attend. I said I would, as long as she promised me that she would keep herself in check. She said she would.

I went to the meeting with the three moms. The two other women handled themselves appropriately and civilly. Unfortunately, Rachel's behavior was at the other end of the spectrum. Almost from "make yourselves comfortable," Rachel attacked these women with such offensive vitriol that even I was momentarily dumbfounded. I interceded, telling her to stop. I said it three times, but there was no stopping her. The fourth time I had to yell, "Rachel, stop it!"

Unfortunately, that experience wasn't a one-off. Superficially, Rachel had a beguiling personality, but what lay under the surface was anything but. If not for Lauren and Sasha, whose father had left the country—as it turned out, never to return—and Rachel being pregnant with Alexander, I would have been out of that marriage as quickly as I was in it. But I loved Lauren and Sasha and felt a tremendous responsibility to be a stabilizing paternal force in their lives. I never thought that their biological father, Kevin, who was European, would leave the country, AND his boys, permanently. Gone! Physically, emotionally, and financially. I certainly wasn't going to walk away from Lauren and Sasha, and there was no way I wasn't going to be an ever-present father to my child that was on the way. I'm just not that guy. I was going to be a loving father. No problem. I was going to make the marriage work. PROBLEM. That would be a challenge, but with determination and perseverance, qualities that served me well in my life up to that point, things would get better. At least that's what I was telling myself.

I loved being a daily part of Lauren and Sasha's life. Bottles, diapers, getting up with them in the morning, and bedtime stories. Did I mention sports? Sports, sports, and more sports. Wrestling, football, T-ball, minibasketball. You name it. As time went on, my boys got into skateboarding, bicycle motocross, and snowboarding. Of course there was also just the crazy, stupid shit that boys do. I knew a little something about that too.

IIIIIIIIIIIIIIIIIIIIIIIIIIIIIIII

On weekends growing up, my best friend Duane Clark and I would go to his dad's beach house in Malibu. There we'd get into all sorts of mischief and adventure. Dick bought Duane a go-cart. It was yellow, and we called it the Banana Crusher. We'd take it up to an empty parking lot in Pepperdine and just drive the crap out of it. Then we'd drive it up and down on the street in front of the beach house.

We were like daredevils, little Evel Knievels, always on skateboards or dirt bikes. At the time, there was a show on TV called *Thrill Seekers* with Chuck Connors. Filled with dangerous stunts, the show was like an early version of the X Games. We built a ramp on Duane's driveway out of plywood and stood a couple of two-by-fours on top, laying an additional one across them. Next we took my dad's movie camera and taped it to the dirt bike, making perhaps the first GoPro. We filmed the stunt from the point of view of the handlebars as we crashed through the boards. Next, we lit the two-by-fours on fire, and one of us would lie next to the ramp and film the bike going over and crashing through the flaming wood from that vantage. Duane had editing equipment at his dad's house, so we edited the whole thing together. It was really pretty good for a couple of kids.

We spent one summer fixing up his playhouse, which you'd climb a ladder to get into because the house was on stilts. We put floor tile in and repainted the walls, made it our clubhouse. *The Six Million Dollar Man* with Lee Majors was the inspiration for our next film project. We filmed ourselves standing in the doorway and facing into the playhouse. Then we'd jump backwards, land on the ground, turn to the camera, and walk away backward. When we reversed the film it looked like we jumped up into the fort.

Not surprisingly, I always had stitches or a cast from some stunt, sport, or the martial arts classes I took. Dick and his wife Terry would call me "Dumb Donald." But one time it was Duane's turn to get hurt.

We were always playing games or having competitions, the rules of which simply amounted to how many times we could do something in a row. How many times could we throw the football without dropping it, for instance? This one time, we had a tennis racket and we were hitting a big Nerf ball onto the roof of Duane's house. When the ball rolled back down off the roof the other guy had to hit it back up without letting it hit the ground. There was a bay window on the roof and a couple of times we hit the pane with the ball and left some marks. The next day, Duane's mom told him to climb up to the roof to clean the window. He called me to ask me to come over to help him, which I did. When I got to his house there was blood in the driveway and blood on the steps.

His sister told me that the window broke when he was cleaning it, and he cut his wrist and had to go to the hospital. Duane didn't just cut his wrist; he severed his median nerve and radial artery. They had to perform emergency surgery and he was lucky he didn't bleed out. When he came back from the hospital his forearm and hand were wrapped like a club.

When I saw him, I thought it would be a good idea to make light of the situation with some words of encouragement.

"Look on the bright side," I said. "It didn't happen to me." Duane wasn't amused.

||||||||||||||||||||||||||||

I really enjoyed pint-size roughhousing with Lauren and Sasha, just as my dad had done with me. I also got to strengthen our father-son connection through sports. Lauren was around four when I introduced him to his first Dodgers and Lakers games. I will never forget how excited he was. I had regained some of what I had lost with my dad and brother passing, but there was more to come.

People always say during a pregnancy that they don't care what the sex of the child is, as long as it's healthy. No question that in the big picture I felt that way as well, but I'd be lying if I said I didn't want my firstborn child to be a boy. The entire male side of my family had been taken away, and I'd be damned if I didn't want some of that back. That wish was granted. The ultrasound revealed that Rachel was pregnant with a boy. My heart soared.

Alexander was born on February 16, 1995. It wasn't without some drama. The umbilical cord was wrapped around his neck. From the monitoring devices the obstetrician could tell that it was tightening and releasing. I had previously asked if I could deliver him, and even under those circumstances, thankfully, I was still allowed to. I saw the top of his head, then his face, shoulders, and out he came right into my hands. It was incredibly exhilarating and joyful, but also a bit scary. He was as purple as a grape, and not breathing. In the blink of an eye he was out of my hands and the doctors and nurses were professionally and wonderfully doing their thing. Quickly he was breathing and letting out beautiful cries. The gift of him was truly redemptive for me. When I held Alexander in my hands again it really did feel like a *Lion King* moment. I wanted to hold my Simba up to the heavens for all the world to see. Boy, did I relate to Mufasa in that moment. For me, in that little body was the life force that was taken with the death of my father and brother. Those losses, particularly my father, were made right. I named him Alexander Jael Feinberg Diamont. Alexander after my late maternal grandfather, because I knew how much that would mean to my mom. The initials AJF for my dad, Albert Jack Feinberg. The circle of life indeed.

CHAPTER **10**

||||||||||||||||||||||||||||||||||||||||||||||||||||||||||||||||||||||||||||||||||||||

Spreading My Wings

n 1996, I decided to make a change in my career. I'd been under contract to *The Young and the Restless* for eleven years. The contract was pretty restrictive, and I was feeling like I wanted some freedom. I wasn't unhappy; I just wanted to spread my wings a bit. I expressed this to my boss, Bill Bell Sr. Bill was the cocreator, head writer, and executive producer of *Y&R*. A brilliant and wonderful man. It's not an exaggeration to say that he was a legend in our medium. In addition to *Y&R*, he, along with his wife Lee Phillip Bell, created *Another World* and *The Bold and the Beautiful*. I had had my familial losses during my time on the show, and Bill was very kind and supportive. He was no less so in this circumstance. He gave me his support and understanding. I really appreciated that. He said he was hopeful that I would return, and that he wouldn't recast Brad Carlton; he would instead send him off to Europe.

So I left the show and booked a couple of jobs right away. The first one was a Movie of the Week with George C. Scott, one of my idols. My character, Ray, was very different from anything I'd played before. He was a blue-collar southerner, and not a good guy. As it happened, my first day on the set I was shooting confrontational scenes with George. I must admit, I was a bit intimidated. This was the actor who won the Academy Award for playing Patton! George also had a reputation for being a bit ornery. Well, he couldn't have been nicer or more professional. I introduced myself, and he was incredibly welcoming.

I asked him how he liked to work. Did he want to run lines or just go out and do it? We ran lines, got to know each other, and had some laughs. We were called to the set and did our thing. He was a total pro, but also liked to have fun, which was perfect for me. By the time we were shooting our scenes, I was very much at ease and ready to rock. The problem was that we were on location in the mountains of Virginia in winter, and I was freezing my ass off. I was out on the porch, and George was in the house. It was so cold it was hard to make my mouth move. Seriously. Thankfully, craft services got me some hot tea, which helped thaw my face. Lol! I loved working with George. I couldn't help but think of my dad. He loved *Patton*. We had watched it together. He would've thought it was the coolest thing ever that I was costarring in a TV movie with George C. Scott. On our last day working together, I asked George if he would sign a script page on which we had dialogue together, and an original *Patton* movie poster that I brought with me. He did. That poster still hangs in my house today alongside that script page.

Next thing you know, I added working opposite another Oscar winner to my résumé. This time it was Jack Palance, who won the Academy Award for best supporting actor from the role he played in *City Slickers*. I booked the lead in a low-budget movie called *Marco Polo*.

Working with Jack was a blast as well. It was a very physical movie, and a great experience. The problem was that we shot in Ukraine, and I was gone from my kids for seven weeks. The TV movie had had me in Virginia for a month. As much as I enjoyed the work experience is as much as I hated being gone from my kids. Some actors really enjoy being on location. It kind of becomes its own world where rules don't apply and familial responsibilities are forgotten. That just wasn't my thing. I missed the boys. Alexander was in diapers and changing on a daily basis. Lauren was playing flag football for the first time, and I wasn't there to watch, let alone coach. Sasha was in preschool, and I missed picking him up. On the way home we would often stop at this hotdog vender and get a hotdog and chips. Sasha was really into his potato chips. It became our thing, and every time Sasha got in my car after school, he asked, "Daddy, get little chips?" I started calling him Little Chip, and I'll still call him that today.

After I got home from shooting *Marco Polo* for almost two months, I was booked to play the villain on the season finale of *Baywatch*. We shot on a cruise ship going to Alaska, and in Alaska.

Great experience. Had a good time working with nice people. But I was gone again. Hated it. I missed being with my kids on a daily basis. I wanted to go home. Literally and figuratively.

During my two-year absence from *Y&R* I sent Bill Bell a Christmas gift, as I always had while I was on the show. It was a beautiful antique fountain pen set including the ink. He sent me a handwritten thank-you note using the pen. Among other things, he wrote, "I miss your talent. Just know that *The Young and the Restless* will always be here for you." It was time to see if he meant it. I called Bill and opened with, "I want to come home." He was thrilled to hear it, and I was thrilled with his response. Indeed, he was true to his word. Within two weeks, I was back on the show, and couldn't have been happier...professionally.

In my marriage, I was just existing. Rachel and I were vastly different people, and I had put myself in the mental mind-set and emotional space of maintaining this marriage until my kids were grown. I had heard other people talk about not being happy in their marriage, but staying in it, keeping the family together, for the sake of the children. Hanging in there until the kids grew up. I never wanted to be that person, and yet here I was. Rachel had a personality that required a lot of maintenance. The goal was to keep her on an even keel. It was sort of a walking-on-eggshells scenario.

That was the thread that would run through our marriage. Periods of normalcy, but always waiting for the other shoe to drop. During a lull in the drama, Rachel got pregnant again.

Even with the shortcomings of the marriage, I was overjoyed with the news. I wanted another child, and I'd be lying if I said I wasn't hoping for a boy. That hope would become a reality December 10, 2000, when Luca was born. It was hard for me to wrap my head around it. As much pain as I had endured losing my dad and brother is as much joy as I felt having Luca complete the redemptive circle. My marriage did not yield the same redemption, however.

The addiction and personality issues again became the central theme in our marriage, leading to an untenable situation. My attempts to get Rachel to address her issues with counseling, AA, or rehab were dismissed. Partying with her friends was the priority, and the kids were suffering. Things had reached a breaking point, and I told Rachel that she had to get help or I would divorce her. We got divorced.

Over the course of the divorce mediation, my priority was protecting the kids. Keeping them safe. Rachel gave assurances that she would maintain sobriety. Family court isn't pleasant, and I had hoped to avoid it for everyone's sake. I accomplished that goal during the divorce proceedings. But not long after, the drinking took over and the joys of family court revealed themselves. Those proceedings were ugly and protracted, but I would go to any lengths to protect my boys.

Eventually, as the boys got older, the visits to city hall became less frequent, and finally, unnecessary. It was a battle of attrition. And with perseverance, my boys' emotional strength and strength of character, along with the steadfast, unwavering support of my wife Cindy, we were able to put those challenges in the rearview mirror.

Putting challenges behind you, and keeping them in perspective while you're in the midst of them, is a central theme in my life and something I've really tried to impart to my kids. Feeling sorry for yourself, wallowing in self-pity, is a useless endeavor. A waste of time. I've felt sorrow, but never felt sorry for myself. I've always known how lucky I am. I've lived, and continue to live, a charmed life. That's not to say I don't have my down periods like everybody else. But I don't allow them to take over. I keep a positive outlook the majority of the time. I believe wholeheartedly that *that* attitude has brought great things to my life. And while I have many examples of that, there's none better than the woman I like to call... THE PACKAGE.

CHAPTER 11

Divine Intervention

The first time I saw Cindy Ambuehl, I was walking out of Bill Bell Sr.'s office at CBS. She was one of a dozen or so girls who had come in to read for a part that day on *Y&R*. I came around the corner, and I remember her standing with her back against the wall in the lobby. I said hi as I walked by, and she said hi back. Simple and quick, yet it was like an electric current ran through me, and I could tell she felt it too. Sure, Cindy was a stunning five-foot-ten blonde, but the other girls in the lobby that day weren't slouches either. Don't ask me how I knew that she felt the same way as I did. I just knew.

Twenty minutes later, I was in Bill's office again to read with Cindy. Any doubt about the spark I felt in the hallway was put to rest. That sense of electricity only increased. The chemistry between us was obvious, and Cindy was chosen along with two other girls to screen-test for the recast role of Ashley, which had been originated by my ex-girlfriend Eileen Davidson.

When Cindy came in for the screen test, to say that I was happy to see her is an understatement. I offered to run lines with her in my dressing room. I did not make the same offer to the other girls testing. She took me up on it, and rehearsing commenced. Part of the scene was a kiss, and if you're gonna rehearse, you're gonna rehearse. We kissed, and only kissed, as was appropriate for the scene, but our connection was powerful. I hadn't felt anything remotely like the feeling I had being in her presence since that first time I'd met Ilene Medecin when I had just turned nineteen. The difference was, I wasn't nineteen. I was a grown man, and a married one at that. And Cindy was a married woman.

She was far and away the best actress I screen-tested with, but I would find out later that Bill had already promised the part to Ron Moss's wife. Ron originated the role of Ridge on *The Bold and the Beautiful*. The screen test was just an exercise in futility. Given that Cindy and I were both married at the time, we weren't in a position to pursue anything, and didn't.

Over the next few years, while my marriage was disintegrating, I would periodically bump into Cindy. Each time we saw each other, we felt the same electricity we had the first day we met in the *Y&R* production office. I remember taking the boys to their karate class, turning a corner, and practically slamming right into her. When I was on my two-year hiatus from *Y&R*, I would see her from time to time on auditions, and the feeling between us was always the same.

A casting director paired us together to audition for a show called *Silk Stalkings*. The producer, who didn't know either of us, saw our separate auditions and thought we'd make a good couple on screen. On another occasion, I went to audition for a show called *The Closer* with Tom Selleck. I was sitting in a chair, waiting to go in for a reading, when Cindy appeared out of thin air right in front of me. Before I could even say hello, she leaned down and kissed me on the lips. Right afterward, I got called in for the audition. I asked her to wait for me, but when I came out of the office, she was gone. As if she had been an apparition. This peekaboo period went on for about five years. Five years! Cindy in her situation. Me in mine. She didn't know how unhappy I was. I'm not sure that I allowed myself to fully realize it either, but I was about to.

It was February 4, 2001. Luca was almost two months old, and I was sitting in my den giving him his bottle. The night before, I had thrown a fortieth-birthday surprise party for my dear friend Glenn Rotner. This is the same Glenn I was playing basketball with twenty years earlier, on the day that I was leaving to begin my modeling career in Paris. I had Luca in my lap and was feeding him with my right hand, and was holding the phone in my left hand, laughing with Glenn about some of the events of the previous evening. I hung up with Glenn, and was giving my adorable little boy my full attention. It was a great morning, but that was about to change abruptly, and tragically.

My phone rang. I answered it, and it was my mom on the other end. She was obviously panicked and told me that my niece Alyssa had just received a call that her mom, my sister Bette, had a heart attack and was being transported to the hospital by ambulance. I calmed my mom down as best I could, and told her that it must be some misinformation. She probably was having some chest pains and was going to the hospital as a precaution. I then got my niece on the phone, and she told me she was heading to the hospital. I told her that I was sure that her mom was going to be okay and to be careful driving to the hospital. I told her that I was leaving immediately and would meet her there. I woke up Rachel and handed Luca over to her.

At the hospital, Alyssa, mom, and I awaited news in the waiting room. I went to the nurses' station to ask what was going on, but they didn't have any information for me at that point. I told the nurse that no matter what the outcome, to make sure and give me the information privately. About half an hour later, I was brought into the emergency room, and the doctor walked up to me and said: "We worked on her for about forty-five minutes…" I was sure the next thing I was going to hear was that she was okay, but the next thing he said was: "We couldn't bring her back."

I felt like I had been hit in the gut with a baseball bat. This wasn't possible. It simply couldn't be. I told the doctor I wanted to see her, and I was taken into the OR. The intubation tube was still in her mouth as my sister lay there lifeless on the table. All sorts of emotions washed over me, not the least of which was the dread I felt knowing that I was going to have to tell my niece that her mom was gone. I got my niece and took her into a private room, held her face in my hands, and told her that her mom was gone. I explained to her what the doctor had explained to me, which was that they had done everything they could to bring her back, but couldn't. My niece broke down, and I held on to her as we cried together. That was—still to this day—the hardest thing I've ever had to do.

The coming days were obviously very difficult, but also provided an opportunity for clarity in regard to my marriage. My sister was divorced from her kids' father. He was a limited presence in their lives, and Alyssa and my nephew Drew—who was thirteen at the time—were going to need help emotionally and financially. Rachel and I were on opposite ends of the spectrum on how much responsibility for their care we were willing to take on. It was another nail in the coffin of our marriage.

Sometime after the dust settled on my sister's passing, my phone rang in my dressing room. I answered it, and heard Cindy's voice on the other end. She had heard about the loss of my sister, and was calling to express her sympathy. I was really happy to hear from her, and couldn't hide from that familiar feeling that coursed through my body when being in her company, even over the phone. Maybe we knew each other from another life? Soul mates? There was an undeniable connection. My experience with Rachel after my sister's death, along with the other issues that I've already described, drove home for me that life was simply too short. And, whether Cindy was in my life or not, it was time to get out of my marriage.

Cindy's marriage had dissolved, my divorce proceedings had begun, and five years later we were finally in each other's arms. There was not a doubt in my mind that this was the woman I would spend the rest of my life with. This is what love is supposed to feel like. As I said earlier in the book, I'm a slow learner. You hear the stories of people who get married and divorced three, four, five times. They just keep repeating patterns, marrying maybe slightly different versions of the same person, but the fatal flaws are still there. Not me! I couldn't have got it more right the second time. I'm not the most religious person in the world, but Cindy being brought into my life made me believe in divine intervention.

I call Cindy THE PACKAGE, because she truly exemplifies that expression: brains, beauty, heart, and, most importantly, an incredible sense of humor. Nobody makes me laugh harder than my wife. The fact that she held the SAG record for most situation comedy guest appearances in a year should come as no surprise. She also starred in two of her own shows, *Action* and *Head over Heels*. If Cindy wants to accomplish something, she simply does it. She isn't lacking in perseverance, and has intellect and creative ability in abundant and equal amounts. As striking as she is physically, she always leads with her heart, which is a very disarming quality.

Cindy grew up in Anaheim. Her father, John, was a cop with Anaheim PD for thirty years, and her mom, Sandy, who we recently lost, was a stay-at-home mom. Later in life, she got into banking, and though she only had a high school education, became an executive vice president at both Downey Savings and Universal Savings and Loan. Sandy was also a beauty with a keen intellect and a love of laughter. She and Cindy really were two peas in a pod.

Cindy attended Cal State, Fullerton, where she took a dual major in math and business. *I didn't do that!* While attending CSUF, she paid for school by modeling. She traveled all over the world, probability and statistics textbooks in hand. She was the Budweiser girl. I may be wrong, but I don't think that there are a ton of Bud girls with degrees in probability and statistics. Her success with modeling did more than allow her to pay for school. It also allowed her to invest in real estate. That would be a harbinger of things to come. Her physical attributes provided income. Her intellect allowed her to graduate at the top of her class from the business school at Cal State, Fullerton. But her creative gifts were as yet unfulfilled. That would change with her decision to get into what we call here in Hollywood "THE BUSINESS."

Her love of comedy and innate belief in her comedic skills took her from Orange County to "Hills that is, swimming pools.

Movie stars." For those of you that don't get that reference, it's from the series *The Beverly Hillbillies*. Though Cindy had a successful career as an actress in situation comedies, films, and episodic work, including three years on *JAG*, her love of business and desire to be more in control of her own destiny led to her decision to pursue real estate as more than a hobby. At forty-five, Cindy got her real estate license. I don't suppose this will come as a shock, but today Cindy is one of the top Realtors in the country and a partner at The Agency. She's been acknowledged by the *Wall Street Journal* for her accomplishments and has been named by the *Hollywood Reporter* as one of the top thirty agents in Hollywood. Am I proud of her? Fucking A. I'm in awe of her.

Cindy and I didn't have a run-of-the-mill courtship. In fact, we didn't have a courtship at all. We were in it. Zero to sixty. Cindy was meeting all the boys and gradually being incorporated into our lives. Well before we got to this point, I asked her if she fully appreciated what she was getting into. A challenging ex-wife, all the boys, and general chaos. True to form, she wasn't intimidated. In fact, she said she was all-in. And she was. From day one to as I write this book today, she has been rock solid. A stabilizing force in all of our lives. An unwavering spirit with a heart to match. She would need it!

In the beginning, and thankfully for just a short period of time, there was some resentment on Alexander's part toward Cindy. He liked sleeping in his daddy's bed, and didn't take well to being kicked out. But soon he opened his heart to her, and now they are as close as mother and son can be. Luca, who was a toddler and very attached to me, would wedge himself between Cindy and me, holding his blankey (which he still has to this day) in one hand and pushing Cindy away with the other hand. That stopped as well. Last Mother's Day, on a big chalkboard we keep on the wall, Luca wrote a "why Cindy is the best mom list." Needless to say, that moved her to tears.

Lauren and Sasha's relationship with Cindy at the start was a little more complicated. I guess they had a right to be confused. For all intents and purposes, they had two nonbiological parents. Rachel also harbored some very hard feelings against me, and by extension against Cindy. Lauren and Sasha were bombarded with a disinformation campaign by their biological mother. I'm a firm believer that the truth will set you free, and that turned out to be the case. Soon, Lauren and Sasha could see Cindy as she was, and not as the woman their mother had painted her to be. In a short time, the relationship they had with Cindy would also start to grow. Today, they know they can count on her.

If things weren't challenging enough in this embryonic period of adjustment, we were just getting started. In a nutshell: Cindy had significant fertility issues, and a small window of opportunity in which to get pregnant. As we were navigating our way through an already tumultuous period, we had to find our way through this challenge. Cindy's life was in Orange County; my life was in Los Angeles. She was changing her life dramatically as I was in the throes of a difficult divorce and the complications it presented.

While there was not a question in my mind that I no longer wanted to be in my marriage, it was very hard on me because of the kids.

Cindy had a legitimate concern that when push came to shove I wouldn't go through with the divorce for the sake of keeping the family together. That had, after all, been my mind-set for the course of my marriage. And I was getting pushback from my estranged wife. Cindy expressed that if I was the "donor" and she was fortunate enough to conceive, if I didn't go through with the divorce there was no way that she would have her children with Rachel as a stepmother. While it certainly wasn't remotely a matter-of-fact decision, with all things considered, I agreed. Cindy expressed that her ex-husband Steve was willing to be the donor. He didn't have children, and they were still very good friends. It did take me a day or two to process everything, but once I did, I thought it was a good idea. Actually, it turned out to be a great idea. The in vitro was successful, and Anton and Davis came into the world on January 17, 2003. This is a classic example of "all's well that ends well." Anton and Davis have two loving dads, a spectacular mom, and given the fact that each one of them is six foot three (and still growing) as of the writing of this book, they have four big/LITTLE brothers. And to top it off, Steve and I are great friends.

I'm really proud of all the boys. They have each other's backs, and there aren't any labels. They're all brothers. Not full. Not half. Not step. Just brothers. I don't want to paint the picture that everything was just a walk in the park. There were a lot of adjustments to be made. When I was leaving Rachel, I had a conversation with Lauren and Sasha, letting them know that I was divorcing their mother, but not them. I wasn't going anywhere and never would. Given that their biological father had abandoned them, I was concerned that somewhere inside their emotional lives, they were frightened that I would do the same.

Then, of course, there was the introduction of Cindy into our world while in the midst of the divorce. And now let's add to the already tumultuous mix...hey guys, sit down...Cindy, who you're just getting to know, is pregnant, and there will be two little brothers on the way. It was a lot. No question, there was a great deal to take in. I told them about the fertility problems, the long discussions Cindy and I had about the state of my relationship with their mother and the divorce, and about how the window for Cindy to have children of her own was closing. It's amazing how understanding kids can be when you talk to them frankly and honestly. I walked them through the whole situation, and after our talk, and with some time to process the information, they were really supportive of Cindy through her pregnancy. Once they got over the initial "shock" and Cindy became a much-needed constant and stable maternal presence, we settled into our lives. When Anton and Davis arrived, the older boys were wonderful with them, as well.

We were just your average family. Well, not quite. We were living in two apartments, one on a floor above the other. We were constantly going back and forth between apartments, making sure everybody's needs were covered. If there weren't enough schedules already, now there were infant twins in the mix. It was pretty crazy. I can't say enough about Cindy during this period. With no prior experience, she was instantly a wonderful nurturing mom, not only for her newborn biological children, but for all the boys. She went from having zero kids to being a mother of six boys in what seemed like the blink of an eye. Anton and Davis tied us all together like a bow on the package. Life was sort of a controlled tornado. We were constantly in motion. A blur that moved to and from school, practices, games, and doctor's appointments. Cindy was the Mominator. Thank God that she is the epitome of a multitasker. She was keeping everyone on track, including me. Oh, and by the way…she was still shooting *JAG* and had started a clothing line that she sold on the Home Shopping Network. Did I mention she'd just given birth to twins? I think I forgot to mention, and this was no small part of the equation, that my niece Alyssa had been living with us for a significant portion of the time I just described.

I really liked the building we were in. It was a luxury complex in a great location in Brentwood. I think it held an emotional attachment for me because of the relief I felt when I moved in. Even with everything I was going through at the time, it felt like a sanctuary to me. I went to great lengths to make it a home for the boys, and I accomplished that. But a year later, Cindy and I were more than ready to move out of our dual apartments. We started searching for a house during the height of the real estate market boom in 2004. We must have bid on four or five houses and lost out every time. And there were plenty of homes that we looked at and didn't think were worth the money, or just didn't fit our needs.

Then, Cindy found a house that she thought we should take a look at. It was in Santa Monica Canyon, right near the beach. Great location. As we pulled up to it, I didn't really care for its architectural appearance. I told Cindy I didn't want to go in, but she wanted to take a look. A few minutes later, she came out to the car, insisting that I come in. She said, "It's not great, but it has potential, will fit our needs, and we're in an ideal location." I couldn't argue with that. In fact, I grew up driving through Santa Monica Canyon on my way to the beach, and I spent a lot of time with my brother at the beach. The area appealed to me in a big way. I'm glad she came out and got me, because she was right. We wanted five bedrooms, and it had five bedrooms. But what really sold me were the four fireplaces. I love me some fireplaces! Great location by the beach (I love me some beach), five bedrooms, four fireplaces, and potential. It felt right to us.

The community the house was in was a charming neighborhood with families and people who had lived there forever. There was Paul, a charming man who was ninety-four and walked his schnauzer by our house every day. We became great friends. Peter Graves of the TV series *Mission: Impossible* and the *Airplane* movies lived on our block. So did Barbara Billingsley, who played June Cleaver on *Leave It to Beaver*. We really liked that the area had an old-Hollywood vibe. Not only that, but it also had historical significance. The woman who lived on our corner was 103 years old, and still lived on her own. She knew the history of the Canyon and would beguile us with stories. We came to find out that our house was the watering hole for the Pony Express, and the house down the street was their actual mail stop. So to recap, some cool old-Hollywood types, some charming folks, great family neighborhood, a short walk or two-minute bike ride to the beach, and a bunch of bedrooms and... fireplaces. Perfect! My wife was, of course, right. Our bid was accepted. Our family was complete, and now we had a home. All we had to do was move in... or so we thought.

CHAPTER **12**

||||||||||||||||||||||||||||||||||||||||||||||||||||||||||||||||||||||||||||||||||||||||||||||

Rubber Hits the Road

In the space of a little over a year, the Diamont-Ambuehl clan—which now included six kids ranging from an infant to the age of thirteen—lived in four different places and had moved part and parcel three separate times. We got good at moving. Like a well-trained army decamping.

Yeah, right.

Not long after we closed on the house in the Canyon, we found out that it had well-hidden and extensive water damage. What was initially a nightmare turned out to be a blessing in disguise. The only way to fix the problem was to bring the house right down to the studs, which is what we did. We were able to make the changes that we would have done slowly over time in one fell swoop. But we were again homeless. We moved into two suites in a boutique hotel right on the beach with a Jacuzzi and a pool. The kids loved the hotel, and so did I. We were boogie boarding just about every day. The boys took surfing lessons. But it wasn't the right environment for a nesting mom with two infants. Three months later, we found a rental house where we stayed for nine months.

When we finally moved into our new house, we felt as though we were finally home, and that life would start to settle down.

Cindy went from having zero to seven children in one pregnancy. She transformed into the den mother of a frat house from a single TV star while somehow assembling an incredibly successful career as one of LA's top real estate agents. It's a 24/7 occupation, and yet somehow it took second place to our kids. She shuttled them to school, practice, doctor's appointments, clubs, shopping malls, sneaker stores, and even first dates. She helped them with their homework, listened to the daily drama of their school days, and gave them worldly advice.

Cindy would tell me that I should wear a cape because of my propensity for trying to rescue people. But the truth is, she's Superwoman. Without her, our family would fall apart.

We were like a three-sided box, an open-ended container that was on the verge of spilling out all that we were. And then she came along and sealed us. Cindy is the fourth side of our box. Cindy and the twins have competed us.

The older boys call the twins "the babies." Even when they had grown up and started preschool, they were the babies. The term was more than just endearing. It meant that they believed it was their job to care for and protect them. Which they did. Luca especially liked being the big brother. It was incredibly cute. Luca's hair was shoulder-length at the time, and he looked like a little Tarzan watching over Anton and Davis when they were babies.

Anton and Davis are fraternal twins and are very different both in their physical appearance and personalities. There is a photo of them as infants in which they are looking right into the camera. Anton's eyes are soft, focused, and make him seem like he's happy to be right where he is. It's a very cerebral stare. Davis's eyes, on the other hand, are wide and wild with a devilish grin that says, "Let's get this party started."

Anton looks like his biological dad. Steve comes from a big family. His three brothers are all well over six feet tall. Anton was a big baby who began to sprout into a big kid. But he's like a gentle giant. He loves to cuddle. People probably wouldn't think it to look at me, but we're very similar in our cuddling nature. As a kid, I would wake up in the morning, and walk into the kitchen where my parents were inevitably seated at opposite ends of the kitchen table. I would climb into my mom's lap for a while, and then move on to my dad's.

Davis looks just like Cindy, and I often say that they are the real twins. Davis has a tendency to bounce off the walls, but he's pretty cuddly too. When he and Cindy fall asleep together, watching TV, I'll just stare at their heads, side by side, marveling at how much they look alike. Despite their physical and personality differences, Anton and Davis are as close as can be.

As a baby, Davis developed severe articulation disorder, a rare language delay. Doctors told us that he might not ever speak. When he did start to talk, no one could understand what he was trying to say. No one, except for Cindy and Anton. For the first years of the twins' lives, even up to when they started preschool, Anton served as Davis's interpreter. The teacher would ask Anton what his brother had said. Cindy, meanwhile, set out on a mission to get the best help for Davis that was available. She accomplished that. She found a speech-language pathologist named Wendy Schall, "Miss Wendy," as Davis would call her. Most people have the ability to draw on a vocabulary that they assemble from the words they hear. You find in your head the word you want to say and are able to pronounce it. Davis didn't have that ability. He had to be taught every word he knows, and had to be taught how to say them. Twice a day, for seven years, Cindy or I took Davis to appointments with Wendy Schall. And for many of those appointments, Anton sat quietly in the waiting room.

Anton was so protective of his brother that we began to worry that Davis was becoming too dependent on him. In kindergarten, we separated them. By then, Davis had two years of language therapy and was speaking much better. Cindy tells the story of taking him to his first kindergarten class. The rest of the kids were sitting cross-legged in a circle on the floor. Davis wouldn't sit with them, and instead sat by himself all the way in the back of the room. Cindy encouraged him to move up, but he refused.

"No, Mommy," he said. "I don't want to." He was afraid of the kids not liking him because of the way he spoke.

"But, Davis," Cindy said, "you can speak now."

The next week he scooted closer to the kids, and the week after that he was sitting with them. The bow on this story is that when Anton and Davis were graduating from fifth grade they both gave the graduation speech. Davis is just as articulate as his brother. No quit in that kid. Cindy refused to give up and so did Davis, and Anton too. With Cindy as their coach, the twins formed a little team that refused to be defeated. When I say "team," I mean it. At times, Anton would take over the coaching responsibilities, and it was pretty cute.

He would say to Davis, "Use your new words, the ones that Ms. Wendy taught you."

That's Anton. A kind, caring kid. The gentle giant. A personality trait that belies his size, which is a great quality . . . except on a football field.

Anton and Davis looked up to their big brothers, Alexander and Luca, and wanted to play on Luca's Pop Warner team, the Venice Bulldogs. Alexander was still in high school at that time and was a Venice Gondo, so his little brothers were all about wearing the navy and white. Kids often have an idealized image of football, but when the pads go on and the hitting starts, fantasy goes out the window. It's then that kids find out what they're made of. Anton and another player were the biggest kids on the team. This other boy knew that Anton was his competition, and wanted to make a point of letting Anton know that he was the alpha dog. He wasn't quite as big as Anton, but his attitude and the aggression he brought with it were huge.

I was standing on the sideline during practice with the boys' biological dad, Steve. As dads do, we took note that this other lineman was taking it to Anton. On a break, he walked over to the sideline, and it was easy to see the tears in his bright-blue eyes. He got a double dose of daddying. The gist of it was not unlike the line that Tom Hanks used in *A League of Their Own*, where he was the head coach of a girls' professional baseball team: "There's no crying in baseball." Well, ideally, there's no crying in football. Definitely not when some other kid is trying to whoop yo' ass. Steve and I were trying to help Anton understand that it wasn't that this other kid was bigger or better than he was. He just was being more aggressive, and Anton had to meet his aggression with equal or greater aggression. We explained that this other boy had gotten in Anton's head, and if he just went back out there and brought up his intensity to match his size and strength that the tide would turn. It turned. Anton didn't look back.

After Luca was born, I didn't anticipate having more kids, particularly given the status of the marriage I was in at the time. But then Cindy came into my life, and not long after that, so did

Anton and Davis. I couldn't imagine our lives without them. And I mean that when I say it, especially because of an incident with Davis where I thought we were going to lose him.

||||||||||||||||||||||||||||||

Davis was six at the time. He'd been sick in bed with a virus, and his fever had just broken. I was outside in the pool with the rest of the boys, playing water basketball. Cindy was working and not home. Davis came out of the house and said he felt better and wanted to hang out with us. He looked better, but the poor kid had been really sick. I didn't want to let him go in the pool, but I compromised and told him he could sit in the Jacuzzi for a few minutes, which is attached to the pool, but elevated above it. He wasn't allowed to be in there by himself, so I told Sasha to go in with him, and to keep an eye on him.

Everything was fine…until it wasn't.

All of a sudden, Sasha was screaming for me: "Daddy, Daddy!" Davis had passed out, but Sasha grabbed him and got him out of the water. The panic in Sasha's voice was enough to get me immediately out of the pool. When I did, it was clear that Davis was having a seizure. I took him from Sasha and held him in my arms like a baby. His entire body and face were locked up. His fingers were gnarled. His jaw was clenched. His eyes were open but vacant. He wasn't breathing and was turning purple. The boys were all frozen in place. I yelled to my nephew Drew to call 911.

I cradled him in my arms and just kept saying, "Breathe,

Davis. Breathe. I'm here. I've got you. Breathe, Davis. Please breathe." It felt like an eternity. I thought he was dying in my arms. It was horrible.

Then all of a sudden, he sucked in a breath and, very slowly, his body and face began to relax. Almost at the same time, I heard the sound of the ambulance siren. It felt like it had taken them half an hour, but in reality it was just a few minutes. It's hard to even describe the amount of relief I felt with him taking that breath at the same time that I heard the sound of that siren, and the ambulance approaching.

I carried Davis out to the front of the house. The EMTs started doing their thing, and one of them asked me what had happened. I described it to them.

I jumped in the ambulance, still in my bathing suit and dripping wet. In the meantime, the boys got ahold of Cindy, told her what happened, and that Davis was doing better. She was on her way to meet us at the hospital.

It was an incredibly helpless feeling. In the ambulance, Davis became somewhat responsive, though in an out-of-it way. He was looking at me, but through me. Finally, he said, "Where are we?" Tears welled up in my eyes just from the relief of hearing him speak.

We brought him to the chief of pediatric neurology at UCLA. And that's how we found out how much doctors are in the dark when it comes to seizures.

Davis's legs hurt badly for a couple of weeks afterward and

we often had to hold him in our arms. Cindy really was a mama bear looking after her cub. He wasn't quite himself for a while. He eventually recovered fully, thank God. There's never been even the slightest incident since, and the doctors gave us no reason to believe there would be a recurrence. They also couldn't definitively tell us what happened. The doctors' best guess was that the spa had potentially elevated his body temperature and that there may have been the presence of a virus in his brain, and somehow a confluence of events created the seizure. I gladly accepted the ten years that experience took off my life, to have Davis take that breath and have a full recovery.

One thing I know for sure from the whole episode is how much I love him.

At no time is the worth of someone you love more in evidence than when you think you're going lose them.

iiiiiiiiiiiiiiiiiiiiiiiiiii

I mentioned that I yelled to my nephew Drew to call 911. He wasn't just over for a visit—he had joined the brood. And that wasn't without its share of drama.

Cindy and I took a weekend trip to New York just to get away and have some time together. We had a great time, but when we landed back in LA, things took a turn. I checked my voicemail and there was a message from Drew, who was fourteen at the time. He was crying.

He was living with his father, Marvin, who, as I mentioned

earlier in the book, was a limited presence in his life, and his father's girlfriend. She didn't treat Drew as well as she could have, and I had confronted her and Marvin about it more than once. But this time things had escalated, and on Drew's voicemail he said that he couldn't take it anymore, and to please come get him. That's all we needed to hear. We called Drew and told him to pack his bags because we were on our way to get him. Up to this point, even with the challenges it presented, we had felt it was best that Drew live with his father, and it was what Drew had wanted, as well. So Drew had put up with his father's hoarding and his girlfriend's incredibly unpleasant and sometimes borderline abusive nature because he wanted to live with his dad after my sister's passing. But no more.

That voicemail really threw us for a loop because it was so contrary to Drew's normal demeanor. A tall string bean of a kid, Drew had a perpetual smile on his face. My sister Bette and I used to say Drew came out smiling. He was a very sweet, happy kid. Cindy and I realized that a smile that used to be genuine had of late been used as a cover to hide what he was really feeling. Lost and alone. Cindy and Unga Gunga were about to remedy that. When Drew was little, he couldn't pronounce "Uncle Donald," so he called me "Unga Gunga." Even at fourteen, he would still do that for fun.

What better way to cure feeling lost and alone than to move into a house with six other boys? For Cindy and me, when we were already at six, what was one more? Truthfully, initially the boys were kind of like, "WHAAAT???" It was a pretty full house, but they understood what Drew was dealing with and made him feel right at home. They abused him just like they abused each other.

With the addition of Drew, The Magnificent Seven was complete, though a better Western comparison might be the Cartwrights with Ben, Adam, Hoss, Little Joe, Candy, and Jamie Hunter/Cartwright (a little TV trivia for you!). Then again, *Animal House* with John Belushi might be more apropos.

Drew was actually a dream. When he moved in with us, he was attending Milken, a very large Jewish high school with a very high academic standard. The only thing Milken didn't offer Drew was a basketball team commensurate with his talent—by then he had soared to a towering six foot six.

Though he played for the high school team, he also played AAU basketball and found guys to compete with who were on his level. He excelled in school, found time for extracurricular activities, and even worked part-time at the Adidas store on the Promenade in Santa Monica. In high school, he decided he wanted to be an architect, and he focused all of his energy on that goal. He filled out his college applications by himself, and was accepted and offered a partial academic scholarship at Tulane, where he would attend and go on to obtain a master's degree in architecture. Bette would have been incredibly proud of him. I know I am. He took a tough turn in his life and turned the difficulty into a challenge. He not only overcame that challenge; he went on to accomplish amazing things.

Drew was a great example of what I hope that all my boys realized: In life it's important to recognize your weaknesses and play to your strengths. You are who you are, and you get what life gives you. You can curl up into a ball and feel sorry for yourself, or you can make the choice to grow from the adversity. You can crumble under the circumstances, or turn obstacles into opportunity. That's exactly what Drew did.

And I'd like to tell you that all my boys followed his example. But if I did I'd be lying. By the time Lauren was twelve, the boys and I had seriously been through the wringer. But when Cindy came into our lives it was like a summer breeze. I went from just trying to figure out how to make it from one day to the next to having real joy in my life. On one level, Lauren and Sasha welcomed the structure that Cindy brought to our home. She was mom right away, to all the boys. But even her nurturing presence couldn't make up for the emotional hurt Lauren and Sasha carried. And, although I tried my hardest, I couldn't stem the tide of bad behavior they both exhibited.

The summer before he started high school, Lauren was nervous about not knowing anyone. "Get involved in a sport," I told him. "Those guys will be your friends right off the bat."

I suggested water polo, a mentally and physically challenging sport that would take some serious training to make the team. I saw it as a bonding opportunity for us, something we could do together. I got us a swim coach, and we hit it hard in the pool for a couple of months. WE SUFFERED, side by side. It was good for both of us. He made the team, and some of those guys are still his good friends today.

But out of the pool, Lauren started treading water.

I'm not a child psychologist and don't pretend to be one. I can't tell you in a scholarly way what kind of effect his biological father's abandonment or his mother's drinking had on him—I'm sure the feelings from those circumstances were overwhelming for him at times.

I try to love all my boys equally, and feel blessed to have each one, whether they're mine through blood or not. My connection with Alexander and Luca, however, is also something that is out of my control. We are bonded on an organic level that can't be replicated by all the psychology books and all the family psychotherapy in the world. Although I tried my hardest to treat my relationships with all my sons equally, I'm sure that being the biological father of two of them had an effect on the others, especially Lauren and Sasha.

I remember when Alexander was just an infant and I would sneak into his room as quietly as possible so as not to wake Rachel. I'd put him in his safety seat, carry him out to the car, and take him to Du-par's, a bakery and restaurant that serves the best pancakes in LA. In some ways, those early morning trips were like I was stealing him away from all the rest of them.

Here we were, just him and me. Dad and son, bonded by blood. When he was six, seven, or eight, I had a Honda S2000 convertible and we'd just go out for rides in it. The Honda became our escape pod, our getaway car. He'd say to me, "Daddy, put on Disco Saturday Night," which was a station then in LA. We'd put the top down and turn up the radio and just drive around. Tom Jones would come on, and we'd both sing along to "She's a Lady."

I'm sure my relationship with Alexander caused my nonbiological sons a great deal of inner conflict and anger. Witnessing the natural bond I had with Alexander, how could Lauren and Sasha not believe they were cheated out of what they needed from their biological father?

I tried my hardest to make up for what they missed. Having been lucky in life, I had the wherewithal to give my sons the best of everything. They grew up in a world of swimming pools and snowboarding trips to Big Bear. For Lauren's bar mitzvah, Cindy and I took Lauren and a few of his friends on a trip to Hawaii. He went to the best schools with bright kids who also lived affluent lives. Though there were negatives along with that, the opportunities they were afforded were limitless. And yet you cannot fill emotional wounds with schools or pools or trips.

Sometimes I wonder what it would have been like had I not come into Lauren and Sasha's lives. My friends always tell me that they were fortunate to have me. Still, some of that damage they experienced is simply irreparable, or at least can't be repaired externally. I know. Despite all my efforts to repair them, life with both Lauren and Sasha would prove to be very challenging and frustrating throughout their teens.

Did I have empathy for Lauren and Sasha? Of course. My heart broke for them. But empathy is an emotion that we should visit once in a while. If it becomes your primary emotion, it displaces the reality of the way things are day to day. And day to day, I gave Lauren the very best life I could. But his attitude went from bad to worse.

Without question, the day my dad bought me the Firebird was incredible. It was an experience that I have tried to duplicate with each of my boys with varying degrees of success. Not everybody has the means to buy their sons cars. But if you can afford it, it's a special experience between a father and son. I was grateful to my dad for buying me the car and I told him that just about every day.

In 2006, when Lauren turned sixteen, Cindy and I thought it would be a nice idea to buy him a car.

Yes, he had struggled in school. And yes, he could be disrespectful, especially to Cindy, and very willful. So you might think, why get him a car if he's being such a jackass? Well, he wasn't a jackass all the time. He was a teenage boy and teenage boys go through the jackass phase just as surely as they go through puberty. Plus, the car would come with conditions, including maintaining his grades in school at a predetermined level. He also had to promise to help Cindy and me (mostly Cindy), with the full-time shuttle service that being the parents of seven boys entails. The deal was, he had to be willing to drive and pick up his brothers at practices when Cindy needed him to, go to the store for her, etc.

At first, it looked like Lauren was going to comply. He worked really hard and brought his grades up to an acceptable level. He also promised up and down to help Cindy whenever he was asked.

As I've mentioned, Lauren had a bit of an entitlement issue. Some of this came from the affluent LA environment in which he grew up. He went to school with the children of titans of business and the elite of the entertainment industry. Most of his friends to this day come from very affluent circumstances. More than once I had to remind him that he wasn't a trust-fund baby. So it came as no surprise that when I asked him what kind of car he wanted he quickly responded, "A brand-new Infiniti FX35."

"Okay," I said. "So that's not going to happen."

Joey Schrage, a friend since grammar school, owns a few car dealerships, including Infiniti. Cindy and I went down to see him and found a beautiful three-year-old FX35, a beautiful used car. We threw Lauren a party at a restaurant called Back on the Beach and surprised him with the car. Like I was with the Firebird, Lauren was over the moon. But unlike me, his gratitude disappeared pretty quickly. His grades dropped, and when Cindy asked him to run an errand it would become an issue. I don't know what kind of teenage rationalization or indignation was banging around in his brain. But if he thought that once the gift of the car was given there was no taking it back, he'd made a serious miscalculation.

After quite a few provocations from Lauren and my subsequent warnings that he needed to get his act together—all of which fell on deaf ears—he called one day to tell me that he'd brought the Infiniti in for service and that the bill was $500. I called Joey at his office and told him that Lauren was repeatedly not living up to his end of the bargain, but that he had no problem calling me for the $500 needed for the service. That FX35 was never going to leave the shop.

Instead, Lauren found a basic white Nissan Versa waiting for him. When I say basic, I mean manual roll-up windows. Very practical. Very good gas mileage. Very unswaggy, and Lauren was all about swag. Initially, he thought the car was an elaborate practical joke.

I wasn't joking. And yet Lauren didn't seem to get the message. He rear-ended a stopped Hummer at a light while he was texting and demolished the whole front end of the car, totaling it. Thankfully, he wasn't hurt. When I went to the body shop I looked inside his car and there was a reckless driving citation for going 120 miles per hour. If I wasn't so furious at him, I might have been impressed he got the Versa up to 120. When I got home, I told him that the next vehicle he'd be riding around in was called a bus.

At that point in his life image was everything for Lauren, so having to ride the bus was just about the worst punishment imaginable, and one that you would think would give him pause. It didn't.

Lauren's behavior wasn't the only issue I was dealing with at the time. In the summer of 2006, my mother died of emphysema. Hers was a painful journey from one level of care to the next. She went from an assisted living place in the Valley where she was fully functioning, to the assisted living center with medical care near us in Santa Monica, then on to another nearby facility that included a hospice, all in a matter of months. She died in that last facility. Mom's passing left only Elena and me as the surviving members of my immediate family. Although I am close to my sister, Elena and I are physically separated by eighteen years and the American continent—she's an accomplished poet and a writer, and was married to the late renowned visual artist Alan Uglow.

While I was grieving my mother, I was dealing with Lauren acting out. It got to the point where something had to break.

When Lauren turned eighteen, Cindy and I told him he could have a party at the house with all his friends, just as we'd done for Drew, and take his girlfriend out to any restaurant in the city he wanted. Considering that he'd fucked off to the point that he failed to graduate with his high school class and had to take some classes online to get his diploma, I thought the offer was pretty generous. You want to go to Spago, I said, be our guest. When he told us he'd get back to us I should have known what was coming. After visiting his mom, which didn't help the situation because she tended to fan the flames, he said he went with her to look at houseboats to rent and that he wanted to cruise around the Marina with all his friends, and then take everyone back to a suite at the W Hotel.

Why not hire Kanye West to perform? I thought.

I told him, if he wanted his suite at the W and a houseboat party, bon voyage. But I wasn't paying for any of it.

Lauren got really angry and indignant with me. He said he was dumbfounded by my offer. Dumbfounded? Then he went on the attack. He said things to me that were so disrespectful, I got about as angry as I have ever gotten in my life.

I said, "Lauren, I have given you my heart, my time, my money, everything I have to give, and if this is how you feel about me, get the fuck out." As I said, I was as angry as I've ever been.

I told him, "You need to get out and go to your mother's, where the two of you can sit and have a pity party about what an asshole I am."

"In fact," I said, "If you don't respect me, why would you want to be in my company? This anger, these feelings that you have toward me don't make any sense. This is the unresolved anger toward your biological father and him abandoning you, and you're projecting it on me. Otherwise it doesn't make any sense. All I've done is love you, care for you, and provide for you."

He did move out, and into his mother's place. It didn't take long, however, for him to realize that living in our house was a much better situation. Very contritely, he asked to come back, and we let him, but with stipulations and conditions that needed to be met. Just as he had promised with the Infiniti, he agreed that he would do everything we asked of him.

Talk is cheap. Not long after Lauren moved back into the

house, that same behavior reared its ugly head. I had asked him to do something significant for me. I can't recall what the request was, but he told me that he couldn't help out because of a work commitment. He explained that he was going to be doing some PA work on a commercial production. That certainly seemed reasonable to me, and I understood.

Well, understanding can turn on a dime. As luck would have it—in this case, bad luck for Lauren—I bumped into a friend of his who unwittingly threw Lauren under the bus. And then backed up over him. He told me about what a blast Lauren must be having dirt biking. "Dirt whatting???" If Lauren wasn't covered in mud, he was about to be. I called him on his cell, and not surprisingly, I couldn't reach him. Clearly it was too hard to hold the handlebars and answer the phone at the same time. When I finally did get ahold of him in the early evening, I asked him how the job went, and he told me really well, but it had been a long day and he was exhausted. Given that he was so exhausted, I told him that I felt it was important that he find some place to get some rest. He said he was on his way home, and planned to do just that. At that point, I said, "Well, that's great. After you're done putting your bags in your car you can do that."

There were a couple of moments of silence, and then he said, "What do you mean?"

I told him that I knew that he lied straight to my face and that I was done having Cindy's and my trust compromised. I told him that his bags would be in front of the house.

"Where am I going to go?" he asked. I suggested more dirt biking.

When he came home his suitcase was packed, and on the porch. We had a conversation about him growing up and acting like a man. I told him he should start taking some pride in how he conducted himself. It's easier to talk the talk, but you earn people's respect by walking the walk, and that's an expectation that I express to all my boys.

As my dad used to say, "Don't give me lip service... Just do it."

CHAPTER **13**

‖‖

The Promised Land

In 2008, I marked my twenty-third year on *The Young and the Restless*. During my time on the show, I'd witnessed firsthand how my industry changed in remarkable ways. By then, foundational soaps like *As the World Turns* and *Guiding Light* had started to crumble. Indeed, both shows would be cancelled in 2009. With the demise of *ATWT*, Procter & Gamble, the company that gave soaps their name, no longer sponsored any daytime drama. The advent of reality TV, the internet, DVD sales, TiVo, and five-hundred-channel choices were like parts of a supernova that had exploded in the daytime-viewing universe. And soaps were being sucked into the black hole. In the '80s, the Nielsen numbers were in the teens. Back in the mid-1990s, in the middle of my career, *The Young and the Restless* had Nielsen numbers in the sevens, and by 2006 we were in the fours, which translates into a significant loss of viewership.

Though we had long since fallen from the dizzying heights of popularity soaps once enjoyed, we had leapt light-years ahead in technology. Instead of shooting live-to-tape, cameras were integrated into an editing system that allowed for incredibly quick intercutting. *The Young and the Restless* was the first daytime drama to shoot in HD. Bill Bell also took courageous steps in tackling and exploring needed-to-be-told story lines like AIDS, date rape, assisted suicide, and more. I'm proud to have been part of a talented ensemble of writers and actors who took artistic chances. It was that courage, I believe, that helped *Y&R* hold on to our spot as the top-rated daytime drama, despite the drop in viewership.

Our head writer/executive producer on *Y&R* from 2006 to 2007 was Lynn Lathan. One day Lynn sent me a script, which I read in my dressing room. In it, I found that Lynn was changing the name of the character that I had played for over twenty years from Brad Carlton to George Kaplan. The story line involved Brad having led a secret life because he and his mother were in hiding from Nazi decendants. When I was finished, I picked up the phone.

"So Brad is really George, and Jewish?" I asked.

"Are you okay with that?" Lynn wondered.

"Well, I'm Jewish," I said. "So yeah, absolutely."

⊪⊪⊪⊪⊪⊪⊪⊪⊪⊪⊪⊪⊪⊪⊪⊪⊪⊪⊪

When it came to anti-Semitism, I really was naïve as a child. The grammar school I attended in Encino, California, was almost like a country school. I had the same group of friends from kindergarten through sixth grade, a mix of ethnicity, race, and religion. So it was something of a culture shock when I was enrolled in Brentwood School in seventh grade. Most of the students in Brentwood were from the west side of LA, very affluent kids, and very exclusive. There was a small group of about four or five boys that were exclusive in the worst sense of the word. All of a sudden, I went from being comfortable in an ethnic mix to being called a kike. Instead of Feinberg they'd called me "Feinkike." I remember coming home and asking my dad what a kike was. Even though I had never heard the word, for some reason I just knew it was a Jewish slur.

"It's the worst thing you could call a Jew," he said. "It's like calling a black person a nigger." He had asked me where I heard it, and I said that I'd heard it at school, but I just played it off like it was no big deal. My dad kind of looked at me sideways, but didn't pursue the conversation.

My father's family was about as Jewish as you could get. Joe Feinberg, my grandfather, was a tailor in the Garment District in New York City. My sister Elena tells me he lived in a house with a yard in Brooklyn, made Passover wine, and spoke Yiddish. He was a Conservative Jew. My dad loved his parents, but rebelled against some of the dogmatic aspects of Judaism. I think later in life some of his reluctance to embrace Judaism was because of the anti-Semitism he experienced on the road as a salesman. Additionally, while my dad was raised religiously, my mother—although Jewish—was as secular as a person can be. The result is that I, along with my brother and sisters, weren't raised religiously. In fact, we weren't exposed to Judaism in any significant way. When I was growing up, we didn't celebrate Hanukkah, but we did do Christmas. Not the religious aspects, just the celebratory ones. You know, Santa, Rudolph, the tree, and of course, presents. We didn't do Passover, and though I would stay home from school on the High Holy Days, I had no idea why. My brother did wear a big gold Star of David around his neck, and my paternal grandmother gave me a mezuzah for my thirteenth birthday. I guess that was to make up for the bar mitzvah that I didn't have.

So now I'm in middle school, and being verbally assaulted with religious slurs from this small group of kids on a daily basis. Today, a lot is in the press about bullying in schools, including cyberbullying. It really makes the hairs stand up on the back of my neck for these kids who are the victims of these kinds of attacks, because I experienced it firsthand. There would be days when my mom would drop me off at school, and I would be anxious on the ride there. I remember getting out of the car and watching my mom drive away, and turning to look at the hill I had to walk down to get to the locker area. I would clench my teeth, and my eyes would water because I knew what I was going to have to deal with. And I did deal with it.

I certainly didn't just take it. Periodically, there'd be a fight. On one occasion, a fight broke out during PE. I was a pretty accomplished athlete, which threatened these losers, so when I would get the better of one or more of these guys in an athletic endeavor, that would get under their skin even more. The Jewish guy was giving them a beatdown. As I said, a fight broke out, and what I'm about to tell you would never happen today, but it happened then. Coach Allen, who was a former marine, grabbed me and one of the students verbally harassing me, Tomas, and said, "You guys wanna throw punches, we're gonna do this the right way." By the way, two years before I arrived at Brentwood, it was a military school. So Coach Allen took us to this vacant room and had us put on boxing gloves and said, "Now we're gonna see who's tougher, and after that's determined, there will not be another fight." Little did I know that the time I spent doing some of what I thought were goof-around boxing lessons with my dad would actually pay off. I quickly got the better of that kid, and that was that. Word didn't spread about the private showdown, and parents were none the wiser—that time.

Over the next two and a half years or so, there would be some occasional dustups, but no big deal. Until ninth grade. One day, I'd had a disagreement with my girlfriend, so I was already in a bad mood. I was walking out of the locker room area when one of these other problematic guys was walking in. There was only one way in and one way out, and we bumped shoulders.

He said, "Watch where you're going, you fucking kike."

Two or three years of pent-up anger came out in that moment, and I beat the shit out of this kid. He required medical attention, and I was taken to the administrative office. My parents were called in, and for the first time heard about what

I had been dealing with over the last couple of years. It was one of the greatest experiences, if not the greatest experience, I had with my dad. I thought I was going to get my ass handed to me. But instead, after being told what had happened by the administrator and then hearing what I had to say, my dad took a few seconds of silent reflection, and then began to speak.

"What do you want me to say to my son?" he asked the assistant headmaster. "That he shouldn't have handled it the way that he did?"

He took the position that this had been going on under the administration's nose for an extended period of time, and nobody knew about it, and nothing was done. He looked at who I believe was the assistant headmaster at the time, and said: "If nobody was standing up for my son, I'm proud that he stood up for himself. I would have done the same thing."

I remember feeling so much relief in that moment. I looked at my dad with even more love and admiration for him than I already had. While my parents did their best to shield me from what was going on behind the scenes, I know there were threats of arrest and lawsuits. My dad and my uncle Bob, who was an attorney with a Harvard law degree, took the position that they were welcome to come at us in whatever way they felt necessary, but to understand that there would be a very public airing of everything that led up to the incident. The kids involved in the bullying were from some very well-known families. Where do twelve-year-old kids, particularly in an age well before the internet and social media, learn to be bigots and anti-Semites? They learn it in the home. They learn it from their parents. Suffice it to say that my punishment was a couple of weeks of lunch detention, and the rest of it just went away. That experience would be profoundly impactful and would have a lifelong influence on me.

This reminds me of a story that my grandfather had shared with me. Alexander Diamant, my maternal grandfather, whom I called Poppy and whom Alexander is named after, was a world-class gymnast and an Olympic prep coach. He was also a secular Jew. As a young boy, I was very attached to him. Well into his seventies, he could still do a pretty decent workout on parallel bars and rings. He was in great shape. Never gained an ounce, looked great, took pride in the way he dressed, and still went to work on a daily basis.

One day, when he was a younger man, he was on a Long Island Rail Road train with my sister Elena, heading to judge a gymnastics competition, when someone made an anti-Semitic remark to him. Poppy dropped the guy right there in the train car. I guess with both my maternal and paternal sides of the family, the apple doesn't fall far from the tree.

I was raised without any understanding of what it meant to be Jewish. Whatever your ethnicity and religious background, it's important to have some kind of foundation and understanding of who you are and where you come from. There's a famous song called "Tradition" from the musical *Fiddler on the Roof*. It's narrated and sung by the lead character, Tevye. He says: "How do we keep our balance? That I can tell you in one word…TRADI-TION!" That really resonates with me. Without at least a funda-mental understanding of your heritage, when you're confronted with bigotry—in my case, anti-Semitism—it can be really hard to keep your balance. I felt equal amounts of pride and shame. If I'm going to be completely honest with myself, when I got into mod-eling a year or two after high school and my print agent talked to me about coming up with a name that sounded less "ethnic" (code for Jewish), I jumped at the chance to use my mother's maiden name. Not only did Don Diamant (I changed the second "a" to an "o" for the sake of pronunciation) have a nice ring to it, but it would shield Don Feinberg from the outside world. Create a layer of insulation from my Jewish identity.

Jews have been changing their names, or having them changed for them, since at least the time of Napoleon. From what I understand, Diamant had once been ben-Abraham. By Napoleon's decree, Jews had to adopt European names or the French state would assign them one, sometimes as a derisive indication of their perceived wealth (Goldstein, for instance), or as a way of identifying them by profession. Pop followed the Diamant family tradition by apprenticing as a diamond cutter in the Netherlands. When he came to the States he went from blue collar to white collar, so to speak. He started as a cutter and later opened his own shop on 47th Street in the Diamond District in Manhattan. By the end of his life he was a diamond consultant and appraiser and once marked a very large stone on *The Mike*

Douglas Show. The story goes that Pop kissed star Elke Sommer, who was also a guest on the program.

"All you people kiss," he supposedly said to the Swedish bombshell. "And I want mine." Apparently, Elke was more than willing. That was Poppy. A lover and a fighter. Hmm...can't argue with genetics.

When I asked my dad about using Diamont instead of Feinberg, he was okay with it. He was well aware that it was common for Jewish performers to change their name for image purposes. He grew up with movie stars like Tony Curtis a.k.a. Bernie Schwartz, Kirk Douglas a.k.a. Issur Danielovitch, and Lauren Bacall a.k.a Betty Joan Perske. Non-Jewish stars like Rock Hudson a.k.a Roy Harold Sherer and Cary Grant a.k.a Archibald Leach weren't immune either. Italians would suffer from the "ethnic" label as well: Dean Martin a.k.a Dino Crocetti, and Sophia Loren a.k.a Sophia Scicolone. But it's a funny thing about pendulums; they swing both ways. And over time, my Jewish identity, and people being aware of it, became my priority.

A conversation I'd had with my dad when he was dying about why he hadn't imparted any of his knowledge about Jewish history or the traditions of Judaism to us really started me down that road. He expressed a tremendous amount of regret that he hadn't given us that gift. A year and a half later when my brother was diagnosed with brain cancer, he felt a strong desire to be bar mitzvahed. He asked me if we could do it together, and I of course said yes. The problem was that he couldn't retain any of the information because of the tumor. I promised him that I would make good on the bar mitzvah for both of us. A couple of years later, I began to study in earnest, and at twenty-nine, I had my bar mitzvah at the Stephen S. Wise temple. The ceremony was presided over by Rabbi Zeldon, a very respected man in the reform Jewish community, and someone who would become a dear friend. Seventy-five people came, including some of my castmates from *Y&R*, my close friends, and my extended family, including my uncle Bob, my dad's brother.

As I stood on the bimah, I was filled with pride at having kept my promises to my dad and brother. It was a really emotional and fulfilling experience. It's funny how things work out. The life experience that I brought to my bar mitzvah at twenty-nine years of age was night and day from what my bar mitzvah would've been at age thirteen.

I am enormously proud that Drew, Lauren, Sasha, Alexander, and finally Luca all stood on the same bimah as I did and became bar mitzvahs. Luca's bar mitzvah was especially meaningful because it closed the circle that started with me. I took the regret that my dad had expressed over not exposing me to the traditions of Judaism, and made up for it six times over. I have no doubt that he was watching over all of us and was filled with pride and appreciation. Although we're not dogmatically religious, the boys are all proud Jews. Alexander even has "chai" tattooed on his left shoulder. If I forget to light the Hanukkah candles on any given night, Luca reminds me without fail. It means a lot to me that Cindy, Anton, and Davis were present for all the bar mitzvahs, and on the bimah right alongside me for Alexander's and Luca's ceremony. Even though Cindy isn't Jewish, she, along with Anton and Davis, embraces all of the traditions just as we embrace theirs. That's how this blended family throws down.

CHAPTER **14**

||||||||||||||||||||||||||||||||||||||||||||||||||||||||||||||||||||||||||||||||||||||||||||||||||||

Never Say Die

I relished the opportunity that Lynn Lathan's story line presented. Any feelings I had into my late teens with regard to insulating my Jewish heritage from the outside world had long since disappeared. Lynn Lathan's story line unfolded like this: Brad Carlton, opportunist, business climber, ladies' man, would reveal that his real name was George Kaplan and that his mother, Rebecca Kaplan (played wonderfully by Millie Perkins, who portrayed Anne Frank in the 1959 film *The Diary of Anne Frank*), had been imprisoned in a concentration camp where she was forced to catalog art stolen by the Nazis. When she escaped, she embarked on a Simon Wiesenthal–like crusade to bring the war criminals to justice and return the art to its rightful owners. In doing so, she made powerful enemies that forced young George and his mother into hiding and to change their identities.

The story was powerful and perhaps gave birth to the first major Jewish character in daytime drama. It was certainly the first time Judaism was explored so deeply on a soap.

I relished the opportunity because my maternal cousins had been imprisoned in Auschwitz. One of them had gasoline injected into his heart as part of a "medical" experiment. In addition, the role gave me the chance to play a nonstereotypical Jewish TV character. Brad Carlton was an ex-Navy SEAL, a tough, strong, virile, psychologically interesting character. Other than being a SEAL, I identified with him. Throughout my life, there have been people who were surprised that I was Jewish, as if I didn't fit into the "Jewish" box that they had constructed. I definitely didn't fit the stereotype. So playing the role gave me the chance to be as out in the world as a Jew as I could be. I did a whole bunch of interviews, several of them in Jewish publications, and the response to them was terrific. Integrating George Kaplan into my character was one of the most satisfying periods of my career on Y&R, and would prove to be my last gratifying experience as an actor on that show.

There is a certain amount of anxiety among the cast anytime a new head writer is hired. Even actors who play core characters can feel uneasy. The reaction is understandable. A new writer might not be as creatively invested in a character as the previous writer was, or might want to bring the story in a direction that doesn't include the character. You also might even negatively remind them of an ex-husband or an ex-wife. The possibilities were endless, and over my career, I'd witnessed a lot of upheaval from the introduction of new writers. But in 2007, when *Y&R* hired a new head writer/executive producer, I was the one in the crosshairs. This time the core character was mine, Brad Carlton, and the scripts I was handed made him into a one-dimensional asshole just for the sake of being one. Initially I thought, okay, let's see where this is going. But it became clear that it was going nowhere. There was no motivation behind the character's behavior, and no explanation.

I'd been on the show for over twenty years and wasn't just going to stand by and watch Brad Carlton walk the plank. On several occasions, I asked for an explanation of the motivation of my character's actions. I wanted to be able to understand why I was playing what I was playing. The explanations I received were vacuous. I heard, "You'll understand as the story evolves" more than once.

What I began to understand was that my character was heading for a dead end that turned out to be quite literal. On the day before we broke for Thanksgiving, my sense of foreboding turned into a reality. I'd just finished shooting my scenes when the stage manager came up to me and told me I was wanted upstairs in one of the executive producer's offices. I knew right at that moment that I was about to be fired. I stopped in my dressing room, called Cindy, and told her the same.

"I'm about to get fired."

"No matter what happens," she said, "Just hold your head up."

I went upstairs, walked into the office, and sat down. It was quick and to the point.

"Don, we're not going to renew your contract."

"Why?"

"We don't know what to do with your character."

"After twenty-three years, you don't know what to do with my character? Would you like some suggestions?"

A Sony executive was present who is renowned for his lack of people skills and was either stupid enough, or enough of an asshole, to tell me: "There is some good news. You're going to die a heroic death."

I'm lucky I didn't pop a blood vessel restraining myself from leaping out of my chair. I had a history with this executive. Not long after this clown arrived at *Y&R*, I was renegotiating my contract. We had just about come to terms on my deal on the same day that we were having some sort of celebration on the *Y&R* set. I was about to return to my dressing room when I saw this exec purposefully leave a group conversation he was in to head my way.

He walked up to me and said, "Hi, Don. So I hear you have seven sons."

Up until that point, he hadn't said one word to me since his arrival on the show. I looked at him oddly, and said, "Yes, I do."

"That's a lot of kids," he said.

I responded, "Yes, it is."

And he said, "Well, it's nice to meet you," and walked away.

It was an interesting send-off given that he didn't actually meet me. Within an hour or so, I received a phone call from the attorney handling my negotiation telling me that he'd received a phone call that he'd never experienced in all his years of practice. The business affairs representative from Sony reneged on their latest offer, and called to say that I could take the original offer or leave it.

So this asshole approached me at the party just to remind me that I had a lot of mouths to feed, as if I didn't already know.

The meeting of my firing ended on a somewhat acrimonious note, and I walked out the door. Happy Thanksgiving! I found out what a turkey feels like.

I was shell-shocked as I walked out of the offices and down the hall to the elevator. I pushed the down button, and was waiting for the elevator when I looked up and at the other end of the hall saw the sign for *The Bold and the Beautiful*. In that moment, I thought to myself, *fuck this. I'm not gonna sit around and feel sorry for myself for even one moment. I'm gonna go look for a job.*

I walked over to the reception desk in the offices for *The Bold and the Beautiful*, and asked if Brad was there. I was told that he was, so I asked to see him. Brad welcomed me into his office. He had been in a conference call with his cohead writer, Michael Minnis, whom I had known from the time he was a page wearing a red coat at CBS. Brad jokingly said to Michael, "Hey, Mike, we'll get Don Diamont to defect from *Y&R* and come to *The Bold and the Beautiful*! Ha ha ha." Brad hung up with Michael and asked me to have a seat.

"What's going on, Don?"

"*Y&R* just fired me and I need a job."

Brad was dumbfounded.

"What do you mean, they just fired you? You're one of the most popular characters."

I said, "Well, they did."

Brad said, "Well, maybe Brad Carlton can cross over to *The Bold and the Beautiful*."

I replied, "Well, that will be a challenge since they're killing him."

He was even more shocked than before. We continued to talk, and I was somewhat emotional. I told Brad that I had a handwritten note from his father that said, among other things, "*Y&R* will always be here for you." That was obviously not the case. Not with him gone.

Anyway, we talked further, and Brad wanted to find out if they were really married to killing the character. He was really sensitive to what had just happened and told me to try and have a good Thanksgiving, and that he would call me on Monday. I left his office grateful for the time he'd given me and our conversation. There are moments in life that are just instinctual, where conscious thought takes a back seat to a survival mechanism. Where this instinct comes from I'm not sure. Are you born with it? Good parenting? A combination developed along with life experience? Wherever the intuition comes from, it has the power to save or at least change the direction of your life. When I think back to that moment, I can't help wondering what my future would have held had I stepped into the elevator instead of walking down the hall toward the sign for *The Bold and the Beautiful*.

I thought about my dad on the drive home. I now had insight to how he must have felt when he was fired from Donmoor, a boys' clothing manufacturing company that he had worked for for thirty years. He was the West Coast vice president of sales until a new president was brought in. I believe the new president's name was Mitch Porigow. He had formerly been at Levi's, and brought his own guys with him. In Dad's case, he was really never the same after that. That was not going to be the case with me. Did I have moments of concern and doubt? Sure. But generally, I had the same level of confidence at forty-six that I had at twenty-six.

I got home and Cindy was wonderful. She was incredibly supportive, and believed the best was yet to come. We didn't share what had happened with the kids at that point. The next day was Thanksgiving and we weren't about to create any sort of discomfort for the kids. We went to dinner at my cousin's house and nobody was the wiser. It was a rough Thanksgiving break processing what had taken place. *The Young and the Restless* had been my home for virtually my entire adult life.

True to his word, Brad called on Monday and confirmed

that *Y&R* was going ahead with their plan to kill my character. He said they were quite a few months ahead in story, but to give him time and let him see if he could come up with anything. I really appreciated it, but that and a dime couldn't get me a Starbucks. It couldn't even get me gas station coffee.

I shot my death scene on *Y&R* the day before we went on Christmas hiatus. In their infinite wisdom, the writers decided that I would drown after rescuing a kid from a frozen lake. An interesting choice given the fact that Brad Carlton was a Navy SEAL. After we wrapped, the cast members threw a party for me on the set and presented me with a watch and some other gifts. It was really touching. Cindy and my kids came. A few days before, I had found the letter Bill Sr. had sent me, the one written with the antique fountain pen I'd given him. "You'll always have a home at *Y&R*," it read. I showed the letter to Brad and he was moved. Though *Y&R* was no longer my home, I would come to find that the cast of the show remained my family. Unbeknownst to me, Peter Bergman, who played Jack Abbott on the show; Eric Braeden, who played Victor Newman; Doug Davidson, who played Paul; Michelle Stafford, who played Phyllis; and Eileen Davidson all called Brad. Peter Bergman told him *B&B* "needs me." Eric went public with his disappointment in *Y&R* for firing me. He called it a "mistake" in an online fan magazine interview. Brad called me to tell me that I had a lot of friends who really cared about me at *Y&R*, and proceeded to tell me about the onslaught of phone calls that he had received on my behalf.

After the holidays, I did what every out-of-work actor does: I looked for work. I hadn't had an agent in years, so I hired one. I started going out on auditions. I also came up with a character and story line for *B&B* and sent it to Brad. But deep into February, there was still no word. There's a blessing hiding under every challenge, and this was no exception. I'm sure that my suddenly being fired created some emotional discomfort for the kids, but it was a great life lesson for them. I was a soap star one minute, and an out-of-work actor the next. I talked to them about my real feelings associated with this sudden change in my life, but they saw me take action, not a bullet. And what turned out to be on the other side gave them a firsthand illustration of why you don't take challenging circumstances lying down.

Sometime in late February I was in the car with Cindy. She had been incredible for the last few months. She was my rock, and did nothing but instill me with confidence when the occasional doubt would creep in. She was and is my real-life Superwoman. She was working, but also a full-time mother with a pair of five-year-olds, a six-year-old, and goofball teenagers, some of whom were acting out in school and elsewhere. She didn't flinch, and she didn't waiver. She was such a stunning example for the boys of what a mom, a woman, can be.

We were riding along when my cell phone rang. I didn't recognize the number, so I didn't answer it. I checked my voicemail, and there was a message from Brad Bell. He said, and I'll never forget it, "Hey, Don, it's Brad Bell. Please give me a call.

Here's my home number." Cindy and I excitedly looked at each other, and I dialed Brad's number. He proceeded to tell me that he had created this character for me named Bill Spencer Jr. He went on to give me an outline of the character.

"So what do you think?" he asked.

"Can you give me a little time to think about it?" I said.

"Sure."

"Okay, I've thought about it," I said. "I'm in."

Brad was thrilled, as was I. I expressed my gratitude to him and we hung up. Cindy and I were overjoyed.

A few days later, I met with Brad, and he expressed to me how invested he was in the success of this character. He told me that he had created some other male characters in recent years that just didn't work. I promised him that I wouldn't let him down. We discussed Bill Spencer Jr. in more detail. I felt like I immediately understood the character, and I also had some strong ideas about his physical appearance, facial hair, how I thought he would dress, and even jewelry. I heard that Brad didn't like men wearing jewelry, particularly necklaces, so I wasn't sure how he'd react to an idea I was going to present. I had a sword necklace that was given to me by my dear friend Tony Giallonardo, who owned a beautiful men's store in Toronto. I talked to Brad about the necklace. I expressed that I felt Bill would wear it because it was representative of who he was and how he approached life. Win at all costs, take no prisoners, fight to the death, etc. Brad like the idea and said to go for it. Little did I know that the sword necklace would become a character of its own. In fact, all the Spencer men wear one.

Given that the death of my character on *Y&R* was still motivating story for that show, and that there were only a few months between my departure from *Y&R* and my arrival on *B&B*, I wanted this new character to look as different as possible from my former role. He needed to be a more fashion-forward kind of guy. Bill was a billionaire media mogul. I saw him as sort of Richard Branson meets Johnny Depp's Jack Sparrow, with a pinch of Hannibal Lecter thrown in, but Bill would only eat people for lunch figuratively.

Brad really liked my fleshed-out vision of Bill. Brad has a wonderfully collaborative nature. He gave me the ball and let me run with it.

It doesn't matter what field you're in: It's one thing to get a job, but it's another thing entirely to keep it. I tell my kids that in everything they do, they'd better bring it. Make themselves indispensable. That is most certainly the case on a half-hour daytime drama with so many talented actors. There's only so much airtime. You'd better make your mark. Make your presence felt. Especially if your character is an island—in other words, not attached to a family. The only familial connection the character had was a half-sister who wasn't a presence on the show. I arrived on the set that first day with point and purpose. There's a new sheriff in town (cue the spurs sound effect). That was the only way to approach it, because that's how I envisioned Bill Spencer Jr.

In May of 2009, I shot my first scene for *The Bold and the Beautiful* opposite Susan Flannery, the Emmy-winning, ball-breaking matriarch of the show. I relished the opportunity, because it allowed me to set the tone for who Bill was right off the bat.

A few weeks later, the audience would see him appear on the *B&B* scene. It was spring, but I didn't want him blowing in like a cool breeze. I saw him more like a hurricane packing 150 mile-per-hour winds. A force of nature who was all about imposing his will in every situation. A guy who lived life with a perpetual chip on his shoulder, and was in a constant state of proving himself. He wanted to bed every woman, and better every man. If he could be that guy—a pirate, but with a charming swagger, wit, and then a vulnerability and beating heart somewhere underneath all that other stuff—we would have a pretty dynamic character, and I would make good on my promise to Brad that I wouldn't let him down.

I knew I might be on my way to getting it right when I received one of the most personally heartwarming and professionally gratifying phone calls of my life.

"Hey, Don. It's Brad Bell, and I am here with your biggest fan, who wants to speak to you."

The next thing I hear is, "Hi, Don. It's Lee Bell, and I am your biggest fan! I just love what you're doing with Bill Spencer!"

I was really taken aback, and told Lee how much her kind words meant to me, and that if I were playing a character with the same name as her late husband, he must be a pretty dynamic guy. I said that I hoped Bill would be proud of what I was doing with the character. She said that she knew he would be, and that she was as well.

Before handing the phone back to Brad, Lee said, "Keep doing what you're doing. I just love it!"

Then Brad said, "Well, there you have it from the cocreator. And yes, buddy, just keep doing what you're doing. I couldn't be more pleased. You're killing it."

If that call wasn't enough, about six weeks after Bill debuted on the show, *Soaps in Depth* magazine selected me as their Gold Star Performer. The review was written by Amy Helmes, and the observations that she articulated about Bill Spencer Jr. were everything I hoped for. I didn't know it was coming. I received a copy in the mail from Eva Basler, our wonderful vice president of communications, with a note saying, "Congratulations, Don! You deserve it!" That acknowledgment from *SID* magazine had nothing to do with ego gratification for me, but everything to do with validation. Validation of the faith shown in me by my wife, Brad, and all of my friends and former castmates from *Y&R* who reached out to him on my behalf.

When I read the review, I got tears in my eyes. It was only about four months earlier that I had been on the cover of the same magazine with a caption that read, "BRAD's DEAD!" Now here I was with this beautiful acknowledgment in the same magazine thanks to Brad Bell having the balls to bring me on to *B&B* while my picture was still being shown on *Y&R*, and story was still revolving around my former character's passing. I have no doubt that he received pushback from the network for creating this character for me, and bringing me on so soon after my demise on *Y&R*.

In November 2009, a year, almost to the day, after I was fired from *The Young and the Restless*, *People* magazine's Sexiest Men Alive issue hit the newsstands, and I was the only actor from daytime included. A couple of weeks later, *Soap Opera Digest* named Bill Spencer Jr. as Best New Character of 2009. A week or two after that, I went to the *B&B* holiday party.

Brad approached me with kind of a cat-who-swallowed-the-canary smile on his face and said, "Revenge is sweet."

I replied, "I don't want to look at it that way. I'm just glad…"

Brad cut me off and said, "No. Look at it that way!"

That cracked me up, and we shared a laugh.

Brad and I shared a lot of special moments in 2009, but none more so than at the Daytime Emmy Awards. *B&B* had been nominated for Best Drama Series. Cindy and I were sitting directly behind Brad and his wife Colleen at the show. There was really no reason for me to feel like I was sitting on pins and needles, except for the fact that I had made a Joe Namath–like prediction in my first meeting with Brad after having signed my contract. I told him that his dad won the Emmy the year I joined

The Young and the Restless, and that the same was going to happen for him now that I had joined *The Bold and the Beautiful*. The crazy thing was, I really believed it. Maybe it was just wishful thinking. Brad had pulled me out of unemployment, and given me the gift of the greatest role I could ever imagine playing. I really did want to see this stand-up guy standing up, with a gold statue in his hands. Plus, his dad had had a shelf full of *Y&R* Emmys for writing and Best Drama Series, and Brad's time for the same acknowledgment was well overdue.

We had reached the final category. Best Drama Series. The moment was at hand. The envelope was opened, and the winner was... *The Bold and the Beautiful*!!! We all lost our minds! Before Brad headed for the stage, he took a moment, turned to me, and excitedly said, "You called it! You're my good-luck charm!" I was absolutely overjoyed! I couldn't have felt more exhilaration if I had won the Emmy myself.

All of us joined Brad onstage, and as I stood there and looked at Cindy in the audience, beaming, I couldn't help but think about how in a matter of months I'd gone from working, to out of work, to working on the best show and for the best boss in daytime television.

The best part about the entire experience was that my boys witnessed all of it. What an extended teaching moment. A life lesson illustrating every positivity cliché imaginable. "When the going gets tough, the tough get going." "You've got to pick yourself up, and dust yourself off." And of course, "When one door closes, another one opens." You're goddamn right! The word "cliché" has a negative connotation, but I see all those "clichés" as truisms. I want my boys to do the same. Failure isn't failure at all. It's opportunity. They saw their forty-five-year-old father fired for something totally out of his control. More importantly, they were witness to my response to it. I was shaken. Knees a little wobbly. But I gathered myself, and came out swinging. Effort and attitude, boys. Effort and attitude!

CHAPTER 15

Little C.H.I.P.s

Though the train was back on track, career-wise, the wheels on the family began to wobble.

As I had with his older brother, I was able to get Sasha into Brentwood School. Parents with means in LA will crawl through shards of broken glass to get their kids into a top college prep school like Brentwood, but what I learned the hard way is that it doesn't mean they should. The school has to fit the kid, and Brentwood and Sasha were not a good fit. Putting your child in an environment where they can feel good about themselves and thrive is infinitely more important than putting them in an uncomfortable situation that they're simply not geared for. In real estate, the mantra is, "Location! Location! Location!" In child-rearing, it's, "Self-esteem! Self-esteem! Self-esteem!" So the goal for Cindy and me was to put Sasha in a place where he would feel more comfortable. To that end, we enrolled him at

Lincoln Middle School, which we thought would provide a better and more targeted educational environment.

Unfortunately, things didn't end up as well as we hoped. He started making friends with some of the "bad" kids. While Sasha was always artistically skilled and interested, his new friends introduced him to graffiti. He defaced the bathroom door with graffiti, an event that necessitated my coming down to the school.

They took the episode very seriously. When I walked into the vice principal's office, there was a police officer standing there. I'd like to tell you it was the last time I saw Sasha in the company of the police. It wasn't.

When we left the meeting at the school, I said to him, "You know, Sash, looks like we have to make some dramatic changes, and we're going to start from the outside in." Sasha was going through a phase of wearing hoodies and covering half of his face with long hair. I took him straight to the Yellow Balloon, a haircutting place for kids. He got physical with me on the sidewalk, pushing me away. But I had him by the collar.

"We can either do this the easy way or the hard way," I said.

Reluctantly, and I mean very reluctantly, he gave in to the inevitable. He had tears in his eyes as he sat in the chair. I didn't order a buzz cut for him because I didn't want to humiliate him. I just told the barber to clean him up. Like I said, I was starting from the outside in.

I don't want to give you the impression that Sasha was a

bad kid.. He wasn't. And we continued to create fun memories and have good times together. For his bar mitzvah we held a huge party in a restaurant down at the Grove, a high-end mall and entertainment complex in LA. We rented a stretch limo and hired a hot DJ and face painters, the whole bit. Afterward, I took him with me to the Indianapolis 500. We rode in the pace car and met (pre-mafia-don-of-cycling-revelations) Lance Armstrong, and other sports stars and celebs. When we were together, just us, it was like I had my Little Chip again. But when Sasha went to high school, things got worse than just graffiti.

Sasha and Lauren went to South Africa to visit their biological father once or twice. Their father had remarried and started another family and had a son and a daughter. By this time, I was talking with Rachel only when it was absolutely necessary, mainly about scheduling for our children, and I wasn't consulted about the trip. Had I been consulted, I wouldn't have been for it. In South Africa, Lauren and Sasha went on a safari and shot BB guns in their father's front yard, all which sounds like a good bonding experience except that it really wasn't. All it did was show them what they could have had, and what they were never going to get, which was a substantive relationship with their real dad. The contact that he maintained with his biological sons in California was minimal, consisting mostly of emails a couple of times a year. One or two trips to South Africa in thirteen years didn't make up for the time in between.

I had a great deal of compassion for what Lauren and Sasha

had to endure. I knew what it was like to lose a father at a relatively young age. But I lost a loving, caring, wonderful man. My loss was physical along with emotional. Their loss was of something they had never had. Instead, they had a father whose actions showed that he cared very little about them, who made a conscious decision to leave them.

As I've said before, I'm not a child psychologist. So I can't tell you how much of Lauren and Sasha's behavioral problems stemmed from being abandoned by their father and their mother's struggle with alcoholism. I'm sure some of the misconduct they exhibited came from the usual teenage rebellion most boys go through. But I can tell you with certainty how frustrating life with Lauren and Sasha was for me at that time. There's only so much thanklessness and selfishness you can take. Did I believe that Lauren and Sasha loved me? Of course. Did I love them? No question. My love was and is absolute. Like? Liking them at that time, now that was a challenge. But as a parent, what I've learned over the years is that you can counsel, advise, and lead by example. But ultimately, it's up to the kid to make his own decisions. I made mine when I was their age, and they were going to make theirs. To learn this, however, a parent might have to get hit over the head a couple of times.

On Sasha's sixteenth birthday, even with the challenges Cindy and I were dealing with, Sasha woke up to a brand-new Altima hybrid with a big red bow on it. It was a sensible car. That he even got a car at all I thought might be a "stay on the straight and narrow" motivator for him. I thought wrong. Remember that hit over the head a couple of times thing?

As it had with Lauren, the car came with expectations. There I was again, taking the car away from my son. Sasha's conduct, however, was worse than even breakneck speeding and rear-ending Hummers. He had been caught smelling like pot at school, and a search of his car revealed marijuana paraphernalia. At this point, the principal had me on speed dial.

The good news was that he happened to be a fan of the show, so Sasha was suspended instead of expelled. When we were walking out of the office, I stopped on the stairs. I didn't yell or even raise my voice, but I was emotional. I held Sasha by his shoulders and looked him in the eye. I told him that the bad decisions you make as a kid get you grounded or suspended. But, as you get older, consequences get more severe. In the worst-case scenario, jail or death. I said, "Sasha, shit rolls downhill. And, your shitball is getting bigger and bigger."

I've never smoked pot in my life or done any illegal drugs. I've been an athlete most of my life, and have always taken care of my body. It also behooves me, given what I do for a living, to keep myself in the best shape possible. But the big reason why I never did drugs is because of what they did to my brother. As you know by now, I loved my brother deeply, but I hated the way he was when he was high. I especially hated his disregard for the people who loved him. I remember one night when I was seven or eight being awakened by my parents and brought down to the car. A girlfriend of my brother's had called in the middle of the night to tell my parents that Jack was unresponsive. Can you imagine a parent getting a call like that? My father drove my mother and me to Palm Springs where Jack was staying. He was just passed out, but for that whole trip the worst-case scenario had undoubtedly formed in my parents' minds.

Because of this, I took a hard line with all my kids when it came to drugs. I'm not so far to the right, or naïve enough, that I don't know that kids are going to recreationally party. Have a beer, smoke a joint, whatever. I'm not opposed to that. Just don't drink or use drugs and drive, I tell them. And don't get into a car that's being driven by someone who's under the influence. Call me instead and I'll pick you up—no questions asked and no punishment. So I'm not inflexible. But I'm also not Snoop Dogg. I don't drop it like it's hot. But I do love the song. The hard-and-fast rule was: no drugs of any kind in our house.

One thing that happens with seven boys is that a grapevine develops. I don't mean to say that the guys are directly ratting each other out (although that does happen when one of them is angry with the other, or out of concern). But information indirectly flows during the normal course of conversation. I started to pick up a few clues along the way that maybe Sasha was selling drugs. Then Cindy and I started to hear things from other parents that corroborated our suspicion. We decided to put a monitoring device on his computer.

I know this is a subject that can cause debate. Personally, I think this whole business about a child's right to privacy is over-blown. We're not talking NSA versus the ACLU here. A parent's number-one job is to protect their kids. With the exception of giving sound advice and trying to teach them right from wrong, you have little control over them when they walk out of your door. Under your roof, however, the roof that you pay for and provide for them, your control should be absolute. In my mind, that includes all electronic devices, and certainly when you're dealing with an extreme situation. Sasha's was getting more extreme all the time. I don't have to tell you that the internet can be a portal to a lot of ugliness, danger, and criminal behavior. We all know that predators prowl the net. Ads on hookup sites and other cyberlistings lure kids into dangerous sexual and business transactions. A seventeen-year-old boy is easily lured, I know. For that reason alone, I think it's okay to monitor your kid's devices.

Does this mean I'm against a kid having any privacy? Of course not. But privacy needs to be earned with good behavior. When evidence starts to mount that your child might be a danger to himself or herself, in our case that your child might be selling drugs, then the right to privacy goes out the fucking window.

So we put the surveillance device on Sasha's laptop and, unbeknownst to him, were able to see who he was talking to. We found out that he was hanging around people he had no business associating with, and that he was selling drugs at beach clubs on the Pacific Coast Highway. When we confronted him, he admitted to selling the drugs. He really didn't have a choice. He was caught red-handed.

Broken record, I know, but boys, actions have consequences. Altima gone. 0 for 2. Fool me once, shame on you. Fool me twice, shame on me. I told him he could skateboard to the bus stop, walk there, ride his bike to school, do whatever he had to do to get around. But he wouldn't be driving the car that I had bought for him.

I think I might have mentioned that Sasha has a stubborn streak. The punishment didn't even put a dent in his behavior.

Soon after I took his car away, I was driving back to my house from somewhere with Anton and Davis in the car. I was just about to turn onto my street when this old 1985 Toyota blew through a stop sign and cut me off. I only had a glimpse of the driver, but a glimpse is all I needed. Sasha! I turned my car around and caught up to him.

"Get home, Sasha. Now!"

It turned out that the car he had belonged to his friend's parents and Sasha purchased the car. Sasha would leave the house on his skateboard and ride to the car, which he parked a couple of blocks away. Cindy and I were furious. Needless to say, he was grounded. Needless to say, it didn't make a dent. And the worst of it was still to come.

As I mentioned, I had made it patently clear to all of my kids that under no circumstance should they bring ANY illegal drugs into my house. I drew a line as clear as can be, one that could not be crossed.

And yet I found marijuana cookies in his room. I can hear you saying, "Okay, so pot cookies. What's the big deal?" The big deal was that they weren't well hidden or secured, and Luca was seven, while Anton and Davis were four. The real issue was that it was part of a much larger problem and showed total disregard for the rules of the house, and his blatant disrespect toward his parents.

I told him that if he wanted to stay in our house he had to go to rehab.

My brother had had a positive experience in rehab. It helped him a great deal. A friend of mine was on the board of a very reputable alcohol and drug rehab center and I was able to pull some strings to secure Sasha a bed. The facility was not a country club like one of those places that you see advertised with swimming pools and curtains blowing in the breeze overlooking a Malibu ocean. Instead, it was a no-nonsense, put-the-drugs-down-and-start-growing-up type of place. Although this was not in the brochure, I was privately promised that the facility was adept at cutting through the bullshit drug addicts tend to spew. I thought the place was perfect for Sasha. His mother, however, did not agree.

"That place is like a prison, and you're not sending my son there," she told me.

I tried to tell her that the ultimatum to Sasha was compassionate, not punitive. Sasha was in trouble and heading for more.

Rachel thought the better idea was to send Sasha to visit her family, who lived near Campbell River, British Columbia. Campbell River is referred to as the salmon capital of the world.

Sure enough, nothing changed after his stay. In fact, it got much worse.

Sasha was home from Canada and staying with Rachel for just a couple of weeks when Cindy caught him shoplifting a six-pack of beer from the supermarket. She was in the car with Anton and Davis, who were little kids at the time. They had their windows open, and heard a lady screaming, "That boy is shoplifting!"

The boys started excitingly telling Cindy, "Mommy, that lady's yelling at Sasha!"

Cindy jumped out of the car and yelled to Sasha herself to get back in the market and return what he had taken. Which he did.

When Cindy told me about the incident, I sat Sasha down and told him, among other things, "If you don't get help, you're going to end up arrested."

Well, call me THE GREAT DIAMONTINI, but a week later I received a text from his mother saying, "Call me asap. IMPORTANT!"

It was bizarre, but I knew right away what had happened. Remember that shitball I had talked about?

Sasha had been arrested for selling pot. Oh, the joys of fatherhood. He was being held in the Santa Monica Police Department jail. No parent wants to hear that their kid is in jail. But, if you had to pick a place for your son to be incarcerated, the Santa Monica Police Department jail had to be on the short list. Although they don't go as far as serving mocha lattes, the lockup is a far cry from the notoriously tough LA County jail. When I arrived at the station, the cop on duty told me that Sasha was alone in his cell. Once I knew he wasn't in with a bunch of gangbangers, I went home. I didn't talk to him—he didn't even know I was there—and I wasn't going to bail him out. Honestly, my first inclination was to do just that, but thankfully my wife is a cop's daughter. Her dad, John Kolbo, was a sergeant with the Anaheim Police Department for twenty-five years. They were both adamant that the only way Sasha was going to learn any-thing was to sit in a jail cell. It was great advice. We saw his pre-dicament as a chance for him to learn what we hoped would be a life-changing lesson.

My phone rang and there was something unusual about the number. Immediately, I knew it was Sasha. I answered, and there was a recording. Something like, "You are receiving a collect call from the Santa Monica jail. Do you accept the charges?"

Sasha was emotional and pleaded with me to bail him out.

I wasn't cavalier about my response in any way. It really broke my heart and pained me to do it, but I told him that if this was the life he wanted to lead, he should feel the full weight of this experience. I said that being in jail at the Santa Monica Police Department was a country club compared to being in the LA County lockup, let alone a federal penitentiary, and that if he didn't clean up his act that's exactly where he could end up. I drove the point home by telling him, and I don't want this to read in any way comedically, that he was way too good looking and not remotely tough enough to spend a single day in prison. He knew exactly what I meant. When I had initially spoken to his mother regarding Sasha's predicament, I told her that I would get a criminal defense attorney.

The next day, Cindy and I went down to see him. Rachel happened to be there at the same time. Sasha could only have two visitors, but the supervising cop was nice enough to let the three of us see him.

Just like on TV, he was behind a Plexiglas partition. With tears in his eyes, he picked up his receiver.

After she was done, I took the receiver, and the first words out of my mouth were, "Sasha, I don't want you to worry. Within ten minutes of my walking out of here you will have a criminal defense attorney. That's a promise."

If Sasha knew anything about me, he knew that I was consistent. If I made a promise, good or bad, I was going to keep it. We talked a bit further about the obvious and then Cindy got on the phone and had a *keeping-it-real* but loving conversation with him.

True to my promise, as soon as we walked out of the jail I called my family law attorney and asked him to recommend a criminal defense attorney. It just so happened that my lawyer was a member at the Equinox Century City gym with a locker right next to one of the most renowned criminal defense attorneys in the country, Harland Braun. I called Harland's office and told his receptionist who I was and briefly explained the situation. I never expected to get Mr. Braun himself on the phone, but about thirty seconds later *he* was on the phone.

To be honest, I fully anticipated him to be a pompous ass. Boy, was I wrong.

"Hi, Don, this is Harland Braun. How can I help you?" I couldn't believe it and told him how much I appreciated him taking my call. I explained the situation in detail.

On top of his brilliance, Harland is a wonderful, grandfatherly type of guy. He told me he would handle the case, told me how he expected it would go down, and gave me his opinion on how he thought I should handle it as a father as well. He said that I should absolutely not bail Sasha out, and that no family should show up at the arraignment. He would be there with Sasha, and beyond that, Sasha should stand before the court on his own.

To put it in perspective, I want to include some Wikipedia

biographical information about who was representing my little El Chapo. Harland Braun is

> a Los Angeles, California criminal defense attorney. His cases have included successfully defending John Landis and his co-defendant George Folsey, Jr. in the *Twilight Zone* manslaughter trial, defending Rep. Bobbi Fiedler against bribery charges, successfully defending state criminal charges against one of the officers charged in the Rodney King beating who was convicted in the subsequent federal trial, and defending several officers in the Rampart scandal. Braun withdrew himself from representing Robert Blake at his murder trial when Blake gave a television interview against his advice. Other celebrity clients have included Roseanne Barr, Gary Busey, Chris Farley, Lane Garrison, and Dennis Rodman. (Wikipedia)

Pretty badass. Homie doesn't play! And on top of that, he said, given the simplicity of the case (simple to him), he would only charge me $5,000 and would represent Sasha from beginning to end.

He was able to get the charges reduced to misdemeanors, but Sasha couldn't violate the terms of his three years' probation, which included community service.

After Sasha was released, we went to Harland's office together. Harland has a kind but commanding presence. When he talks, you listen. As we sat there, Harland said much of the same things that I had said to Sasha about the consequences of following the path he was on.

"Trust me," Harland said to Sasha. "You don't want to be in prison."

But coming from the man at the top of the criminal defense food chain, the information seemed to really resonate with Sasha. Three days in an eight-by-eight walled cell, eating balcony sandwiches, with your only entertainment being whatever book they threw at you, didn't hurt either.

<hr />

I could see the look in Sasha's eyes as Harland was speaking those words, and I knew I was witnessing a turning point.

The hardest lessons are the best. Sasha had to regularly check in with his probation officer and complete his court-ordered community service, which included working at a morgue. Harland also insisted that Sasha reimburse me for the legal fees. It was all about taking responsibility for the situation he found himself in, presently and going forward. Harland and I had spoken before this meeting so we were definitely in lockstep.

Sasha's arrest was an absolute blessing, and he would tell you the same. Without it, it's pretty scary to think about where his life might have ended up. There's not an ounce of shame in what Sasha went through. The shame would've been if he hadn't learned anything from it. It's a cautionary tale for anybody who wants to go down that road. But in my son's case, it was a happy ending. I was so thankful to be able to get back to not just loving my son, but liking him again. And there's a lot to like about my Little Chip.

||||||||||||||||||||||||||||||||||||||||||||||||||||||||||||||||||||||||||||||||||||||||||||||||||||||||

CHAPTER 16

Diary of an Undersized Division I QB

S ize doesn't matter?

||||||||||||||||||||||||||||||||||

Sports were certainly a bonding experience with my dad, and the same held true with me and all of my boys. With Drew it was basketball. Now, I do have one hard-and-fast rule: I'll play one-on-one with all of my sons until I think they can beat me. Then it's time to shut it down. It's very important to retire undefeated.

The tipping point with Drew came when his skill set caught up to his six-foot-six frame. With Lauren it was snowboarding. I got him going, but it didn't take long for him to leave me in the powder. Today, the aerial maneuvers that Lauren can pull off are really impressive, and he's definitely the best boarder of the bunch.

With Sasha it was tennis. I had played number one on my high school tennis team, so I was thrilled when Sasha really got into the sport in high school and made the tennis team. I really enjoyed banging the ball around on the court with him and going to his matches. He got good enough to start giving me a run for my money.

Lauren and Sasha also played flag football in grammar school. I coached Lauren's team, and in his sixth-grade year we won the championship in the closing seconds on a diving fingertip catch that Lauren made in the end zone. It was a great season and a really special moment for us.

I might not be the athlete I was when Lauren and Sasha were little, but Anton and Davis are both basketball players and I love to get out on our court and bang around with them. Or maybe I should say get banged around by them. With both of them fourteen years old and six foot three—well on their way to six foot five—sometimes it requires me to play dirty. A skill I am not afraid to use, and have honed over many years.

I often think of my dad when I'm playing with or watching all the boys participate in their various athletic endeavors. As I mentioned in Chapter 7, my dad was a big football fan and we watched a lot of games together when I was a kid, so I know he would've especially loved the passion and exceptional talent that Alexander and Luca have for the sport.

When Alexander was an infant I called him "my cuckoo bird." He was so wide-eyed and inquisitive. He would pull himself up in the crib and look all around, like a quarterback checking out a blitz package. He really did have an affinity for the game from very early on. I have a photo of him as an infant that I used in a montage at his bar mitzvah, which shows him crawling around the floor with a football. As young as three or four, he was throwing a Nerf football in the hallway at CBS Studios, where my show was shot.

He started playing flag football when he was five, and even at that age was beginning to show an extraordinary talent for the game. It wouldn't take long for him to be on my ass about playing tackle football. I was really on the fence about it. He was about ten years old when we were playing catch with my friend Ed Skelly. Ed's vocation is deputy attorney general for the state of California. But his avocation and passion is football in general, and the art of quarterbacking in particular. Ed had coached high school football for many years, and as we were throwing the ball around that day he made the comment, "You can't teach the way the ball leaves Alexander's hand." The die was cast. That was all Alexander needed to hear.

"I told you, Daddy."

Yeah, he did. It's not that I didn't know it; I just wasn't sure that I wanted my skinny ten-year-old playing tackle football regardless of how talented I thought he was. So much for that. Ed sent us to quarterback guru Steve Clarkson. That relationship would be fortuitous because Steve's right-hand coach was Angelo

Gasca. Angelo was the head coach at Venice High School, and had quite a reputation for sending his quarterbacks to Division I schools. More about that later.

At eleven years old, Alexander was playing tackle football for the Westside Bruins in the highly competitive Valley Youth Conference. They had a kid who had been their quarterback for three years, and Alexander didn't feel that he was getting enough reps to fairly compete for the position. I didn't tell him that, but he wasn't wrong.

One day after practice, he walked up to me, pulled his helmet off with tears in his eyes, and said, "Daddy, it's not fair. I'm better than Chase but they're not giving me enough reps."

Even though I wanted to say, "I know those fucking coaches aren't giving you enough reps, and you are better than that, kid!" I kept those thoughts to myself. Out loud, I said, "Chase has been their starting quarterback for three years. You think you're gonna show up here and get handed the job? That's not gonna happen. You're gonna have to take it. You better just shine with the reps you're given and not waste time feeling sorry for yourself. Just keep working hard, Alexander. Control what you can control. The cream always rises to the top."

ııııııııııııııııııııııııııııı

He was promoted to starter before the season began. Half of our kids had never played tackle football, but we made it to the playoffs as the lowest seed with an even record. We were still finding our stride, however, and the experience that Alexander had gained over the season was invaluable. We surprised everybody, making it to the finals. The championship game was against the perennial powerhouse that had been undefeated for two seasons, the Mid Valley Titans.

The night before the game, the team got together to watch film. Over the course of the season, I had gotten close with the Bruins' wonderful head coach, Willie Green. After watching film, I asked him if I could address the team. I made the point that the Titans were overconfident bullies, and the best way to fight a bully was to punch them in the mouth right off the bat.

Did they ever. From the very first snap our guys were bringing it. It happened to be the hottest day on record in the San Fernando Valley, and Alexander had croup, which is a severe respiratory infection. You'd never know it. He played with a passion and intensity that would be his trademark in high school and throughout his college career. He threw two touchdowns, and at a crucial point in the game, we were at fourth down with twelve yards to go.

The team went into a wildcat formation with our star running back, Willie Green Jr., in shotgun, and Alexander lined up at wide receiver. Willie threw a pass to my son, who left his feet and flew parallel to the ground with outstretched hands, making the catch, landing on his back for the first down. We won the game 20–7 with the Titans only scoring in the last minute of the game. For various reasons, we only had fifteen guys for that championship game. Fifteen tough guys who brought it on every play. What a team!

I had been so sure we were going to win it all that I had T-shirts made up that read: "Westside Bruins, Valley Youth Conference Champions." A few minutes before the end of the game, I opened the box and started throwing them to all the parents. Everybody was blown away. Remember I mentioned Coach Gasca? He was there, too. That wasn't the last special moment Angelo would share with the Diamonts.

Like Lauren and Sasha had before him, Alexander attended Brentwood School. As I mentioned, Brentwood is an excellent college prep school with a solid sports program for its size. But it's not a launching pad for Division I football players. Alexander's prowess as a youth quarterback, and dream to play the position at the DI level, meant we would have to make a move. And move we did. Though we could have gone to any number of LA football powerhouses, we decided the best thing for Alexander's future as a quarterback would be to play for Coach Gasca. That would mean attending what is lovingly referred to as "the ghetto by the sea," Venice High. That would be a very dramatic change of environment from the insulated private school experience.

Just south of Santa Monica, Venice, California, got its name back in the early 1900s when a tobacco magnate carved canals in the seaside town to make it look like its Italian namesake and gin up the property values. Although the canals are ornamental for the most part, they did inspire the most unique mascot name in all of high school football—the Gondoliers.

Venice is a varied and culturally colorful community. There's nothing like the Venice Boardwalk. You definitely see it all. A mix of surfers, artsy types, gangbangers, you name it. Over the last several years, it has really begun to transform. Parts of Venice that were once gang infested have become very tony.

The high school has quite a history too. If you've seen the movie *Grease*, you've seen the school. Virtually the entire movie was shot on campus. Fans of the film are constantly showing up at the school and taking pictures in the same football bleachers, posing as John Travolta. The opening scene of the movie was shot right in front of a bronze statue of a woman with an outstretched hand that Myna Loy posed for when she was a student there. Venice High is a diverse public school and there are rough elements to it. As I said, ultimately we decided on Venice because of its coach. Angelo Gasca counts among his quarterback progeny J.P. Losman, a high school All-American and later a starting QB for the Buffalo Bills.

Coach Gasca was thrilled to have Alexander. I didn't give the rough nature of the school a second thought. As a high school basketball player, I sought out pickup games on the Venice Boardwalk courts. Many times, I was the only white guy in the game. It made me a better basketball player, and the cultural exposure was invaluable. I believed the same would hold true for Alexander. I knew he wouldn't be intimidated by the environment.

Just before he started practicing with the team, he shaved his head almost to the scalp.

The haircut was his way of saying, "Bring it on."

Alexander was on the varsity team as a freshman, though he was played very sparingly that first year. As a sophomore, he found himself in a situation similar to when he first joined the Westside Bruins. A senior on the Gondoliers who had paid his dues was the starting quarterback. If Alexander wanted to start, he was going to have to take the position from him.

The team played Harvard-Westlake in the first game of the season. Though a top-notch college prep, and the school of choice for the children of LA's business and Hollywood big shots, Harvard-Westlake was a rung or two below the football talent level of the Gondoliers. Even though Alexander was a backup and it was entirely possible that he wouldn't play, he was friends with quite a few kids on the Harvard-Westlake team, and kids who attended the school, so the game meant a lot to him.

"We can't lose to Harvard-Westlake."

For us, the game was supposed to be more or less a tune-up to prepare us for the regular season and our more formidable foes. But the next thing we knew, the Gondoliers were down 21–0 in the first half.

With four minutes to go in the half, Coach Gasca pulled the senior starter and put Alexander into the game. He immediately completed a fifty-yard pass to the four-yard line. Then, with seconds remaining in the half and on fourth down, he scrambled and dove across the goal line. He came up strutting and pounding his chest, and the team was all over him. At the time, he was 140 pounds soaking wet, but had and has the heart of a grizzly bear.

In the second half of the Harvard-Westlake game, Alexander was under center. The Gondoliers recovered an onside kick in the final seconds and Alexander threw a touchdown pass to our star receiver, Gabriel Marks, and won the game. Gabe was Alexander's best friend on the team. As a sidenote, Gabe would go on to get a scholarship to play at Washington State where he set the Pac-12 reception record, and is still one of Alexander's closest friends today. From that moment on, Alexander was Venice High's starting signal caller.

Being the starting quarterback and being the leader of the team, however, are two different things. Being a leader requires focus, among other things. You can't have distractions during the season. And what could possibly distract a fifteen-year-old kid from his life's passion? Hmmm.

Alexander had a girlfriend. And I know from experience, if you have a woman in your life, she better lift you up. But she was dragging him down. Here was a kid who already had the world in his pocket, a star athlete with model looks and megawatt personality. Where'd that guy go? South.

As Coach Gasca said, "The only thing I have to compete with *that* is Friday-night lights, and Friday only comes once a week."

One evening, I was in the bathroom and heard Alexander lamenting to Cindy about some nonsense involving this girl. I'll admit, I have a temper, but I generally keep it in check. Generally.

I came out of the bathroom saying, "I can't listen to another second of this shit. Where did my son go? Do you even have a half a ball left, or did they just get sucked up into your abdomen?"

Though Cindy wouldn't have expressed her feelings the way I did, we were in total agreement. I told him that his girlfriend had no interest in supporting his goals. Her only interests were self-serving.

I don't know what Dr. Phil would have said about that moment, but my words were impactful and we started seeing glimmers of a reballed Alexander. That relationship would be on and off through high school, but he wouldn't lose himself again.

Alexander would be challenged that year in another way, as well. He saw one of the linebackers emerge from a secluded area on campus smoking a joint before practice. He confronted the teammate in the locker room, telling him, "I don't want you getting high before practice. This is our year. Our goal is to win a championship and that's not gonna help us get there."

Alexander knew that his critique might not be well received. He was right. And he knew he was right when the guy starting taking off his chain. They were about to throw down, and Alexander wasn't about to back down. Even though this guy outsized him considerably. By all accounts, and I heard most of them, Alexander whooped this guy's ass. It was a seminal moment in his high school career. And right or wrong, it solidified him as a leader of the team.

The Gondoliers were league champions my son's first season, but they lost in the quarterfinals for the city championship. By Alexander's senior year, they went to the semifinals, and lost to Crenshaw High School, traditionally one of LA's best high school teams. As a senior, Alexander was named LA City Offensive Player of the Year.

Cindy and I adopted much of the team, and Gondolier pool parties and barbecues at our house became a regular event. These kids were with us all the time. A lot of the players had challenges that our kids couldn't imagine, and we were happy to open our home to them.

I'm very proud of my son's accomplishments on the field in high school. But I'm just as proud, maybe even prouder, of the nonjudgmental way he saw people. He treated them all with respect as long as they treated him that way too. His high school years were a wonderful experience. They opened his eyes to a culture he wouldn't have been exposed to had he gone to one of the other high schools on our list.

Alexander will tell you he had some of the best experiences of his life during his time at Venice High School, and grew immeasurably in ways that he never would have in a more insular environment.

Not long after he left, he had one of the worst experiences of his life.

Keino was taking his pregnant girlfriend to her home when some bangers rolled up on them. Though the gang element in Venice isn't remotely what it used to be, the Venice Shoreline Crips still exist, and so does the Hispanic gang V13. They weren't technically in Venice at the time, but unfortunately the area Keino's girlfriend lived in wasn't immune to gang violence.

"Where you from, Young Blood?" one of them asked.

For some reason, Keino chose that moment to act like a badass, and responded, "Venice Shoreline Crips, bitch."

One of the bullets they shot hit his spine. Keino was paralyzed from the waist down. This was obviously devastating news for Alexander, and he consoled Keino as best he could over the phone. Life goes on, and when Keino's baby was born, he asked Alexander to be the godfather, a request that Alexander accepted immediately.

My son wears his experience at Venice with a tremendous

amount of pride and appreciation. His time there made him a better quarterback. More importantly, he learned life lessons that he'll carry with him always.

IIIIIIIIIIIIIIIIIIIIIIIIIIIIIIIII

Alexander was six foot one and 150 pounds in his senior year of high school. That didn't stop him from being the most prolific scorer in Venice history. Colleges and universities came calling, among them Indiana University. They were a Big Ten school, and didn't do a lot of West Coast recruiting, but they had been turned on to Alexander by quarterback coach Joe Dickinson. He was a friend of Angelo's, and had spent some time working with Alexander over the years.

Coach Gasca asked Joe to take a look at Alexander's junior-year season highlights. Joe was impressed, and got in touch with Indiana's offensive coordinator at the time, Seth Latrell. Next thing we knew, it was February of 2012, and we were heading to Bloomington, Indiana, for an unofficial visit to IU.

We were taken immediately with the charming midwestern college town. It was a cold, clear night and I remember us walking through the Sample Gates and past the limestone buildings and red-brick halls. The campus is one of the five most beautiful college campuses in the world, according to architectural writer Thomas Gaines, and looked like a set for a movie. We drove to see Memorial Stadium, known as The Rock, which was lit up so you could see the huge portraits of IU greats that hung on the exterior of the stadium. Flags were blowing in the breeze. The sight was incredibly majestic. I looked at Alexander, who was staring up at the stadium.

"Imagine playing here," I said to him softly.

He just shook his head in awe. But play he would. As cornerman Bundini Brown would say to my dear friend Muhammad Ali, "Rumble, young man, rumble."

CHAPTER **17**

||||||||||||||||||||||||||||||||||||||||||||||||||||||||||||||||||||||||||||||||||||||||||||||||||||

The Oaken Bucket List

In Bloomington, Alexander and I met the coaches, watched a six-thirty a.m. practice, then toured the facilities and IU's campus. I don't know exactly what our mutual expectations were, but the experience definitely exceeded them. By the time we left Bloomington, Alexander had made up his mind. He wanted to be a Hoosier. I couldn't disagree.

Over Alexander's time at IU, not just Alexander, but Cindy and I, along with the other kids, formed relationships with people in the community that will last a lifetime. We came to love Bloomington and the friendships we made there. People like Dave and Phyllis Green, Adam Estes, and IU's athletic director Fred Glass and his wife Barbara really enriched our experience.

The only hitch in our giddyup in the ensuing months was losing offensive coordinator Seth Latrell. He left to be the OC at the University of North Carolina. As a sidenote, today Seth is the head coach at the University of North Texas, and offered Luca a scholarship after his freshman year at Venice. We loved Seth, and weren't thrilled with the news, but stayed the course. Four months after that unofficial visit, the final rung on the Indiana recruiting ladder was at hand. Indiana football's one-day camp.

In a phone call I had with Head Coach Kevin Wilson, he told me that Alexander was the number-one quarterback on their board. But he wanted to put "eyes on him" in person, and see him compete against the other quarterbacks at the camp.

I'd been at Alexander's side, or on the sideline, since he was throwing passes in flag football. We'd walked hand in hand leading up to this moment, and now he was about to take the biggest step to reach his dream—and I had to be in Monaco for the Monte-Carlo Television Festival and a *The Bold and the Beautiful* location shoot.

B&B is huge internationally, and we have won the Golden Nymph Award, given to the most-watched daytime drama in Europe, several years in a row. Brad wasn't attending that year, and asked me to accept the award on his behalf, which included thanking Prince Albert of Monaco in my speech. Point being, I was stuck.

My friend Ed Skelly stood in for me.

Alexander killed it in the workout, throwing a sixty-yard dime during a one-on-one drill to a streaking receiver in the end zone. When the camp ended, Coach Wilson walked up to him and curtly told Alexander he wanted to see him in his office at seven the next morning.

Alexander called me and told me what the coach had said.

"What do you think it means, Daddy?" he asked.

"Well, given that you flew in from the West Coast, I can't imagine he'd be enough of an asshole to tell you to show up at his office at seven in the morning to say, 'Nice job. Thanks for coming.' But let's see what happens," I told him.

I was playing the calm dad, got-everything-under-control role, but inside I was doing backflips. The Hoosiers had the number-one passing offense in the Big Ten the prior season.

‖‖‖‖‖‖‖‖‖‖‖‖‖‖‖‖‖‖‖‖‖‖

I was just going back to work after we'd broken for lunch during the shoot the next day when my phone rang. For some reason, I had the time difference mixed up. I thought it was three hours earlier in Bloomington than it actually was. So when my phone rang and I saw it was Alexander calling, I said, "What's the matter? You too wound up to sleep?"

Then Alexander said, "Daddy."

"Yes?"

"I'm a Hoosier."

I said, "You're a Hoosier? Wait, what? What do you mean? It's only five o'clock. What are you talking about?"

He said, "No, it's not, it's eight."

"Eight? You had your meeting? He offered you?"

"Yes! I'm a Hoosier!"

It's hard to put into words what feeling coursed through my body at that moment. Tears just sprang to my eyes. All the years, all the coaching, all the workouts, all the throwing drills, all the arm-strengthening drills, all of the travel camps, all of our conversations, had come to fruition.

We talked for a few more minutes, and then I immediately called Cindy. She had the same reaction that I did. The tears were flowing. The fact is that Cindy was just as important to Alexander's achieving his dream as I was. She was at every game, and a constant supporter. There were many weekends over the years when I wasn't around because of Alexander's football obligations. She definitely made her sacrifices. And now our son was the recipient of a full-ride scholarship to one of the finest public universities in the country, and achieved his dream of being a Division I quarterback. A Big Ten Division I quarterback. Wow!

If all that wasn't enough, it was June 12, Cindy's and my anniversary. Alexander chose number twelve to wear on his uniform as our present. It was a hell of a gift.

Indiana wanted Alexander to come a semester early so he could acclimate to college life, become familiar with the football program, and settle in before practice started in earnest. I knew college would be a transition for him. In December of 2012, he was a senior at Venice High School, and the Los Angeles High School Offensive Player of the Year. In January of 2013, he was going to be a scrub.

For the average kid, a first semester away at school provides a lot of challenges. Some kids go into a shell, hide out in their dorm rooms, and hate the experience. For others, freshman year is no rules, no parents around…time to party. I knew without a doubt that Alexander wasn't going to hide in his dorm room, but I didn't expect him to be Bluto from *Animal House* either.

Before he left, I sat him down.

"For all intents and purposes, you're a professional athlete. Your scholarship is your form of payment. Conduct yourself like a pro. Freshman or not, it doesn't make any difference. You're a quarterback. By definition, a leader. Handle yourself accordingly. All eyes are going to be on you. Got it? Okay. Good. Glad we had this chat."

A couple of months later, I woke up one morning to a text message that consisted of a photo of my son with a gash under his left eye, and blood running down his face. Not to mention the chipped tooth. I didn't think he tripped and hit the edge of a door. Clearly, he'd been in a fight.

Needless to say, I called him immediately, and he explained that he had been at a party with a couple of girls from his dorm. He received a call from one of his other female friends who also lived in his dorm, and asked him if he would come pick her up at a party that she was attending. She said she felt uncomfortable there and wanted to leave. He said sure, and headed over to get her with his friends. Now, the last thing Alexander should have been doing was going to the frat house of a bunch of drunk frat boys. The way social media is today, the frat boys knew everything about my son: that he was a highly touted freshman quarterback, that he was from LA, and that his father was a soap opera star, etc. None of that information made them any more hospitable.

Alexander's coaches had made it perfectly clear to him and the other new players on the team to steer clear of frat parties. Apparently, football players and frat parties can be a combustible combination. The coaches knew what they were talking about.

Alexander got there and he went inside to get his friend. The girls stayed in the car. He found his friend and was leaving with her when some of the partiers started hurling insults at the girl. Alexander defended her. All of a sudden, he was surrounded. Next thing you know he was hit in the face with a bottle of Smirnoff, and jumped.

It rocked him, but he focused on the guy that hit him and came out swinging. Then several guys jumped him. They had him on the ground, at which point the girls in the car had run over and started screaming to let him go.

Alexander describes it as a weird moment, but his shirt had been ripped off him in the altercation, and it revealed his chai tattoo that he had on his shoulder, and one of the guys yelled out, "Wait a minute, our quarterback's Jewish?" Turns out it was a Jewish fraternity. The onslaught ceased. Alexander staggered back to the car and called some of his teammates, telling them that he'd been jumped.

The cavalry arrived in about two minutes. His boys jumped out of their car, yelling, "Who hit him?! Who hit him?!"

The tide quickly turned, and an ass whooping ensued.

I wasn't at all happy with my son. Alexander was told not to go to the frat house, and to make matters worse, he'd been dumb enough to go by himself. He had put a $300,000 scholarship in jeopardy by getting into a fight, and that's bad enough. But things could have turned out even worse. He could have been hurt even more badly than he was, including losing his eye. Someone else could have been hurt badly as well. As it was, he had taken a good beating.

When the head coach found out about the fight, he wasn't happy either.

"Maybe we should sign up some of those frat boys for the team," he said.

A couple of uneasy days followed. The fight happened on the eve of the Little Five, a legendary bike race and weeklong party on the Bloomington campus. Alexander spent the Little Five in a dark room because he had gotten a concussion from being hit by the beer bottle and was now sensitive to light. I sent him a long text about having done the opposite of what I expected. I wrote that I was more disappointed than angry and reminded him that he was in the 1 percent club. That's how many high school athletes receive full-ride college scholarships. At the quarterback position, the percentage is lower than that. The opportunity he now had was something he had worked for his whole life. I also said that he had not only gambled his scholarship, but disregarded what I had expressed to him concerning the fact that while he was away at school he wasn't just representing himself, but all of us, and that his actions reflected poorly on us as a family. I ended the text by saying that if he had to learn his lesson the hard way, then fine, as long as he learned it. I closed as I do any chastising text to my boys, with "I love you, your dad."

A few weeks later, the coach called him in for his review before heading into spring break.

"Here's what we know about you so far, Alexander. You like to drink beer, chase pussy, and run your mouth." Quite a sendoff.

My son came home soon after. It was good to have him back. There's a time to lecture your child and there's also a time to focus on loving him. During that late spring and early summer, his family and friends surrounded him. I don't mean this in a sappy, Hallmark-card way. There were no campfires or "Kumbayas." The brothers gave him a razzing when he came home, but it was just what he needed. I could literally see his attitude change.

In spite of his ADD, when Alexander sets his mind to something, he has a laser-like focus. I saw a look in his eyes in the days before he returned to school that was reminiscent of a time a few years back. Just before he started high school, he had gotten a buzz cut that brought the hair on his head down almost to the scalp. The haircut was his way of saying, "I'm all business."

He did the same thing before heading back to Indiana. He got rid of the David Beckham cut, and just buzzed his head.

Cindy and I knew he was turning a page.

Alexander had learned his lesson but lost none of his fight. My son is a linebacker in an undersized quarterback's body.

His first season at Indiana was supposed to be a redshirt year for him. That meant he could practice and travel with the team without using up any of his four years of college eligibility, and in fact, it would give him a fifth year of football eligibility, and if he so desired, another year of tuition paid for if he chose to get a master's in his field of choice.

Redshirting is not an unusual practice for freshmen, and especially freshman quarterbacks. It allows them to get acclimated to the offense, get bigger in the weight room, and do so without running the clock out on their college career. For Alexander, everything was going according to plan. He was feeling comfortable with the pace at which he progressed.

Then, in the sixth game of the season, Nate Sudfeld, the number-one quarterback for the Hoosiers, separated his shoulder and was out for the year. Along with being a big blow to the team, Sudfeld's injury meant that Alexander would lose his redshirt status and be moved up to the active roster as backup quarterback. Then Sudfeld's backup, Chris Covington, was injured in a game against Iowa. He'd played some of the game with a torn anterior cruciate ligament, a season-ending knee injury.

In the blink of an eye, Alexander went from redshirt freshman to the Hoosiers' starting quarterback. The first game he started was against Michigan State, the fourth- or fifth-rated defense in the country at the time, defending Big Ten champ, and a team with as good a chance as any to make the final four in the College Football Playoff that year.

If that wasn't enough pressure, the game was the Hoosiers' homecoming and would be nationally televised on ESPN. To make matters even more interesting, there was also something called a polar vortex that had descended on Indiana. Alexander thought the ocean breeze in Venice was chilly. He was out of his element in Bloomington—literally.

I talked to or texted with my son every day. Over and over, I imparted the same message to him: "Stay within yourself. Don't try to be anything you're not, because what you are is plenty. Just make sure you bring your focus and your passion, and everything will be fine."

Meanwhile, I was a nervous wreck.

As the game drew closer, the pressure only got worse. *The Crimson Quarry*, a Hoosier Twitter feed, dedicated a whole page to Alexander that practically anointed him as the savior, not only for the Michigan State game, but for the whole season. This praise was in spite of the fact that you could count the number of snaps he'd taken with the first team on one hand, and his preparation for the Michigan State defense amounted to watching one hour of film.

Savior? My son weighed 157 pounds. I was hoping he didn't get killed.

Cindy and I flew up to Bloomington for the game. I sent him this simple text: "Stay calm, and have fun." I should have sent the same text to myself. And then, like out of a dream, the moment he had waited, hoped, and planned for just about all of his life was in front of him. All those days and nights on the football field, all of those practices and camps, and all of that one-on-one instruction led up to this one moment.

And for all of that time, I had been with him. When he was just five, Alexander would sit with me on the couch as we watched the college football highlight shows on ESPN.

"You just keep doing what you're doing," I'd tell him, "and that's going to be you someday."

And now, that someday was here. I couldn't believe it.

Alexander would later tell me that the game was so much faster than what he was used to. Even if he had had the opportunity to practice with the squad or to scrimmage against the first-team defense, he still would have been a step behind everyone else on the field.

He said that probably the most startling moment he experienced that day had nothing to do with the speed or talent of any player on the field. Indiana University had the largest Big Ten JumboTron scoreboard in Memorial Stadium. Alexander obviously hadn't given that any consideration until one play when he was in shotgun, and the live feed went up on the JumboTron, and all of a sudden he was looking at himself as a giant. There was his face, as big as a mountain, looking back at him. It took him half of a second to shake off the surprise. He later said to me that it felt as if his heart skipped a beat.

And yet nearing the end of the first half, Indiana was down by only four, with Alexander leading the offense on drive. On first down and goal, he faked to running back Tevin Coleman and pulled the ball into his midsection while darting to the end zone. The ESPN cameras caught Cindy and me jumping and hugging like crazy, my red Indiana football hat knocked sideways on my head. Alexander pointed up to us and we pointed back. Later, a reporter for ESPN came up in the stands to interview Cindy and me. Maybe for the first time in my life I was tongue-tied. Luckily, Cindy had my back as usual and told the reporter how much Alexander and I are alike.

"Donald sneezed and Alexander came out," she said.

I didn't care about the interviewer or the national audience. My thoughts were all about my son. After he scored the touchdown, I saw him talk to the referee. Later, he told me that he had asked the ref if he could have the ball he scored with.

"After we use it for the extra point," the ref told him.

The next day, when we met Alexander at Memorial Stadium, he was carrying the football. He handed it to me and gave me a hug. On the ball he'd written, "Indiana vs. Michigan State. First DI touchdown. To Daddy, love Zander. More to come!! October 18th, 2014."

As you might imagine, that ball is one of my most prized possessions.

The second half of the game didn't offer the emotional highs the first half had. The Hoosiers sputtered on offense. Alexander made some poor throws, and a couple of passes that should have been caught were dropped. His team ended up getting beaten pretty handily. But the loss didn't diminish one bit of the pride I felt in my son. I didn't need a jet to fly back to LA; I could have done that all on my own.

The thing about playing Hoosier football is that you get used to being the underdog. Indiana belongs to the Big Ten Conference, so they play teams like Ohio State, Michigan, Penn State, and Nebraska. Alexander had to learn his position as starter against the best teams in college football. As far as learning curves go, the next four games were about as tough a curve you can get at his level: Michigan, Penn State, Rutgers, and Ohio State. Alexander started to hear some boos from the fans, but shrugged off the derision and showed flashes of what he was capable of: scrambling away from would-be tacklers and throwing on the run.

Though the Hoosiers lost four games in row, for all of which Alexander was the starting quarterback, we played fairly well against Michigan and narrowly lost to Penn State. He threw a beautiful touchdown pass against Rutgers and we gave Ohio State, the national champions that year, the scare of their lives. Against the Buckeyes, with the Hoosiers down 14–0, Alexander broke free for a fifty-three-yard run that turned the game around and made it a contest.

Top athletes talk about the game "slowing down." What they

mean is that the brain begins to process the extremely fast-paced stimuli and the information that comes at them rapid-fire. Alexander would tell me later that it was during the game against Ohio State when he started to feel comfortable. Joey Bosa was then Ohio State's premier defensive player and is currently the defensive end for the Los Angeles Chargers (of course there's only one real LA football team, and that's the Rams). At six foot six and 275 pounds, Bosa had the speed of a point guard. On one particular play, Alexander was in the shotgun and Bosa came at him unblocked. My son was able to make the subtlest of fakes that left the big defensiveman teetering like a '60s muscle Chevy up on two wheels. Instead of a head-on collision, Bosa was only able to sideswipe Alexander, who completed the throw. Later in the game, Bosa exacted his revenge with a vicious hit on my son.

"He smoked me," Alexander would later tell me with a grin.

But that hit, too, was a turning point. The smile on my son's face was familiar. I'd seen the same smile when he played Pop Warner and during his high school career. It was his "hit-me-as-hard-as-you-can smile" that indicated that it didn't matter how big or strong or fast the other player was or how hard he hit him, my son was going to get right up and get in somebody's face.

There were some crucial drops on third down in the second half. Alexander threw a couple of picks and the Hoosiers lost the game. Still, I believed that Alexander had turned a corner. I might have been one of the few who did.

Over the losing streak, Alexander heard the boos grow

louder. The blog that had had such an unreasonable expectation of my son quickly turned against him.

The pressure on Alexander to win was immense.

On the one hand, this was uncharted territory for me as a dad. My son was in a position that few fathers witness. On the other hand, what Alexander was going through was no different than a hundred other situations that he had experienced. There were just more people watching him than usual.

So I told him what I tell all of my kids: "If you see it, you can achieve it. Keep thinking positively and good things will happen."

Each year, Indiana plays Purdue for the Old Oaken Bucket, a rivalry game that dates back to 1925. Similar to the Army–Navy game, a win against the hated rival could save even a winless season. Cindy and I had planned to go to the game together, but she ended up having a commitment to her parents that she couldn't compromise. So Luca and I flew up to Bloomington.

At halftime, things didn't look good. Down by six and playing poorly, the team provided little for the hometown crowd to cheer about. I'd spoken to Alexander about the importance of keeping up his level of play in the second half of games. Specifically, I said that what he had experienced in the four games leading up to that final matchup prepared him for what was going to happen against Purdue. I had predicted that he was going to have to make a fourth-quarter comeback. And here we were. It was such a great experience for Luca. He was a twelve-year-old quarterback watching his big brother play in this storied rivalry game.

Alexander orchestrated scoring drives on five out of the last six times the Hoosiers had the ball against Purdue, drives punctuated by a couple of beautiful throws from my son and some great runs by our backs.

"Daddy, this is crazy! This is exactly what you said would happen!" Luca exclaimed in the stands.

With 2:20 left in the game and the score tied, Alexander had the team on Purdue's one-yard line. Coach called a time-out, and the stadium around me was a wall of sound—everybody was screaming at the top of their lungs. I was emotionally drained and weak-kneed. I just sat down. I already had tears in my eyes in anticipation of him scoring because I wanted it for him so badly. The boos that he'd heard, all the criticism in the blogs and local papers, all of the negative things being said around campus had to hurt my son. Alexander is a tough kid with thick skin. But he was still a college freshman, after all.

I had seen Alexander pull the ball and run it into the end zone many times dating all the way back to his Pop Warner days, and I had a sneaking suspicion that that was what was coming. The coaches didn't know it was coming, but I did.

When the time-out ended, I got to my feet. The team lined up in a shotgun formation and Alexander took the snap. The play called for a handoff to the running back, D'Angelo Roberts. But Alexander noticed the defensive end pinching in so he could clog the middle. Instead of handing off to Roberts, Alexander pulled the ball, tucked it under his arm, and leaped into the end zone. His teammates swarmed him. The stands went nuts. Luca and I were jumping up and down, hugging each other, and fans were slapping us on the back and running over to high-five us. The feeling I had was nearly overwhelming.

As the final seconds ticked off, Luca and I went down to the field and found Alexander. It was incredibly emotional. Our joy was immeasurable.

There's a photo of Alexander, Luca, and me with the trophy bucket, and Alexander and I are kissing it.

The photo that got the most attention, however, was taken a little later. One of the assistant ADs, Mark Deal, who bleeds crimson and cream, handed Alexander a cigar in the locker room. The picture, which he posted on his Instagram account, showed Alexander still in full uniform with the lit cigar clamped in the corner of his mouth, and holding the Old Oaken Bucket. That was an FU to Purdue, and his Joe Namath moment.

The photo went viral throughout the college football universe. However, the campus had been smoke-free since 2008. So the image of the football team's star QB lighting up a stogie might not have sat well with university officials, and definitely didn't sit well with his head coach, who would ream Alexander in front of the team for having done it. But when I bumped into IU's athletic director, Fred Glass, his comment was, "It's about time somebody brought some swagger to the Indiana football program. That's what we need around here." Kudos to you, Fred!

A couple of days after that last game, Alexander and I were

talking about the season, and he told me that while he had been dealing with the challenges that had presented themselves, he had reflected on his recollections about how I had handled being fired. He said it allowed him to keep things in perspective and to just keep moving through it.

He said, "You're right with what you said about failure. Failure isn't failure at all. It's opportunity knocking."

Wow. Wait, he heard that??? Mission accomplished.

CHAPTER **18**

|||||||||||||||||||||||||||||||||||||||||||||||||||||||||||||||||||||||||||||||||||||||||||||||||||||||||||||||||

Little Big Man

It was the fall of 2005. The night before his first game of organized football, Luca laid out his uniform on the floor—shorts, socks, shoes—as if he were wearing them. He's not much different today. That's who Luca is. Nothing if not organized.

If you had asked me right then, I would have told you that Luca might jump into the outfit and run right out the door and into a huddle. That wouldn't quite be what happened.

Just like his big brother Alexander, Luca started playing flag football in a park near our house when he was in kindergarten. Luca's always been an organized, analytical kid. Although very different in temperament from Alexander, Luca shares his brother's enthusiasm for the game. Both of them would rather play football than anything else.

The next day, Luca couldn't wait to get to the field. Until we got there. We were walking toward the field, and Luca froze.

"I don't want to play," he said to me.

"What do you mean, you don't want to play?"

"I don't want to."

"You couldn't wait to play. You laid out your uniform on the floor last night!"

Ahead of us, the sidelines to the field were lined with parents, family, and friends of the players.

"All those people are going to watch me," he said.

My son wore an expression that was close to abject terror. For a second or two I didn't know whether to hug him or drag him onto the field. Cindy was with me, so we figured if we could get him to the sideline where he could see his friends, he'd change his mind. In theory, a good idea. In practice? Not a chance. He just refused to play.

"Okay, shmook" I said, as I put my arm around him. "We'll skip it for today."

As we walked from the field to the car, I noticed that he looked back over his shoulder.

By the next game, he was completely over his fear and played. He had to experience the fear to get through it.

Right from the start, just like Alexander, I knew Luca had something special on the football field. Actually, I knew it when Luca was around three, and Cindy and I were at the park with him. He was running across the field, not just kicking a soccer ball, but controlling it. With both feet.

Cindy and I looked at each other, and I said, "That's pretty special."

A couple of years later, you could see the frustration on the faces of the kids who tried to catch him. He has exceptional speed and quickness. Even at the age of five, he showed an innate ability to get himself out of trouble on the football field. And I wasn't the only one who saw this. He played against Nikko Gonzalez, the son of arguably the greatest tight end ever to play in the NFL, Tony Gonzalez, who played for the Kansas City Chiefs for seventeen years. Tony called Luca "Little Vick," referring to the former star quarterback of the Atlanta Falcons, Michael Vick, who was renowned for his speed and agility.

When Luca was eight, he began playing tackle football for the Westside Bruins, just as his brother had done. He was the quarterback and starter of the team. We had a game coming up against the team from Crenshaw that was going to be played at Compton High School. That bit of fear that I described earlier was about to rear its ugly head again. Around this time, we were deciding where Alexander would go to high school. The night before, Cindy, Alexander, Luca, and I went to see Venice High School play. Some of the kids at the game knew Luca from the Pop Warner league and asked him where he was playing the next day. When he told them Crenshaw at Compton, they started teasing him.

"Ooooh," they said, "You're headed to the hood, dawg. Better watch out."

I didn't realize it that night, but that impacted Luca.

The next day, when we were in the car going to the game, Luca started complaining about a stomachache. I knew that those were his nerves talking, and I told him that was normal and that he'd be fine when he got to the field.

As we pulled into the parking lot, he said his tummy was really hurting. Again I told him that it would subside. As we were walking toward the field, he said it was getting worse.

In order to get to the field, we had to pass the opposing team, which was gathered together. Luca was already in his uniform.

"There's number eight," the opposing coach yelled to his team as Luca and I walked by. "That's the guy we got to get."

Now I'm thinking, wow, my son's got a reputation. That's pretty cool! But Luca didn't see it that way. His psyche was getting the better of him.

I said, "Let's just go join your team and you'll feel fine."

I told him those guys were just scared of him because they knew they couldn't stop him.

Luca joined his team and I went up into the stands to set up my video camera. I taped all of my kids' games so we could go over the film together. I got my camera up and running. The game was a few minutes from starting when my phone rang. It was Luca's coach.

"Don, Luca won't play."

"What? What do you mean?"

"He won't go in."

"Put him on the phone. Luca, what's this about you're not gonna play?"

"I don't want to play."

"You can't not play. Your team needs you."

"I don't want to play."

"Luca, if you don't play, they'll think you're a scaredy-cat."

Then he got a little emotional. "I don't care if they think I'm a scaredy-cat!"

"Luca, just get in the game. These kids are just like every other team you've played! Just go in for a few plays and you'll see that I'm right!"

Nothing. It didn't matter what I said. He wasn't going to play. That was the glaring difference between Alexander and Luca at the same age. Alexander always wanted to take on the biggest kid. He wasn't scared of anything. Alexander was very much driven by emotion, whereas Luca is more cerebral, and at that moment, he was in brain freeze.

The game started without Luca, and that's how it went almost to halftime. The coach called me again.

"If he doesn't play four plays before the half, he can't play the rest of the game," the coach said. "That's the rule."

"Put him on the phone."

I reiterated what the coach said. "Luca, you're down 12–0. Your teammates are counting on you. You're the leader, and if your teammates think you're afraid, they'll be afraid. If you don't go in now, you can't play the rest of the game."

There was about five seconds of silence on the other end. And then, "I'll go in, Daddy."

You would've thought that it was Tom Brady trotting out

onto that field. The team went nuts; their fans went nuts. On the first play, Luca was in shotgun, took the snap, and ran straight through the middle of the defense about fifty yards. Touchdown. 12–6 at halftime. In the second half, Luca scored again. 12–12. We needed the extra point to go ahead. Luca ran it in, and we beat Crenshaw 13–12.

That was a seminal experience for eight-year-old Luca. He processed the fear, got through it, put it behind him. I don't think it had a damn thing to do with anything I said. Except maybe the scaredy-cat part. Definitely not one of my finer moments, but I felt a lot of pressure to get him to play. Scaredy-cat was the best I could come up with. Luca found his own courage. I was really proud of him.

Luca was born somewhere around eighteen months before I filed for divorce from Rachel. Cindy hadn't moved to LA yet, so I spent a lot of one-on-one time with Luca. He was the sweetest baby and easiest kid. Still is. He would take his nap with his blankey and *susi* (French for pacifier) every day, right on schedule. We'd go to the park, watch *Barney* together, and play games. I'd hold him in the pool. I loved giving him his bath, changing him, putting powder and baby lotion on him. Changing him was the best time for me. It was just such an intimate little thing to do, to watch him coo and start talking, take away his poopy diapers, make him feel better and smell good, get him all cozy in his jammies, and onto his back and happy again. I loved doing that for all my sons.

Rachel's substance abuse had a negative impact on all of the boys, and Luca was no exception. He grew up with promises of sobriety being repeatedly broken, being exposed to some frightening situations, and hours of court-ordered therapy sessions. I'm not going to go into any further detail, but as a result of all this, he cut off communication with his biological mother as soon as he was of an age where the courts held no sway over him.

I'm so grateful that he doesn't remember a life without Cindy, and he considers her "his real mom."

I had all sorts of nicknames for him: "Schmooka la duka," "Lu Lu," and "the schmook," to name a few. One day he went to a party where they were silk-screening hats, and he returned with one that had "the schmuck" written across the crown. I didn't have the heart to tell him. He was so proud of it.

I spent a lot of time with Luca in the pool when he was a toddler. My mom had all of us in the water at six months, and water-safe by two years old. I continued that legacy with all the boys. But Luca outshined them all. He was swimming two lengths of a large swimming pool at two years old. Even before he was kicking that soccer ball I was talking about, his athleticism was on full display.

Luca has the same goal as his big brother Alexander: He wants to play quarterback for a Division I college football team, and he's well on his way. He received four offers after his freshman year in high school, in which he was the only freshman in the city division to be named to the all-city team.

We're back at Venice High with Coach Gasca. How could we not be? Luca wanted to follow in his brother's footsteps, and more importantly, break all his brother's records. Luca definitely had a head start on accomplishing that, given that he started as a freshman, and threw twenty-one touchdowns at 2,300 yards. And in the off-season, he trained his ass off in preparation for his sophomore campaign. But he was about to be tested in a way that we never imagined.

The weekend before the season, Luca asked me if he could go to Palm Springs with some of his friends. I hesitated a bit, and talked about it with Cindy, and we decided to let him go. I was the only one home when he left the house on Saturday, July 22, 2017. Before he walked out the door, I hugged him, and said, "Don't do anything stupid." I didn't want a call from a cop telling me that my son was a statistic. He said he wouldn't. I hugged him, I kissed him, and off he went.

Cindy had gone down to Orange County to spend some time with her dad, who was dealing with health issues. Anton and Davis were in Orange County as well, spending the weekend with Daddy Steve, and Alexander was with his athletic director.

My cell phone rang at twelve-thirty in the morning. At first I thought it was my alarm, but I looked at the phone and saw Luca's picture. I had a little jolt of concern as I answered the phone, saying, "Everything okay, Luca?"

But instead on the other end was an unfamiliar voice, asking, "Is this Donald Diamont?"

"Yes."

"Luca Diamont's father?"

"Yes."

"This is Sheriff Bush, from the San Bernardino Sheriff's Department."

My heart sank.

"Is my son all right?"

"There's been an accident, and Luca's being transported to Desert Regional Medical Center. He's conscious, but has a head injury. Doesn't seem to be any alcohol or drugs involved. I spoke with all of his friends, and everybody's clearheaded and lucid."

He explained that there was a freak accident, and that Luca had fallen off a golf cart, hitting his head in the process.

I was in my car in about two minutes, heading to Palm Springs. I reached Cindy and told her what happened. She was freaking out. She couldn't leave because her father couldn't be by himself, but of course I told her I would call her as soon as I had any more information.

I spoke to the nurse in the emergency room several times on my way down. Luca was taken in for a CAT scan, and it turned out that he had two skull fractures and a bleed in his brain.

I got to the hospital in under two hours, and was incredibly relieved to see Luca sitting up on the gurney. Needless to say, I couldn't hug him and kiss him enough. He was transported to Loma Linda Children's Hospital as a precaution, and spent about thirty-six hours being tested in every way possible.

Everything was negative, and the bleed was small enough that it didn't require surgery. That was the good news.

The bad news was it meant an end to his sophomore football season, and when that news was delivered by the doctor, Luca was devastated, and cried inconsolably.

"My team! My coach!" he kept saying.

The following afternoon, Cindy and I brought him home, which was a wonderful feeling. Obviously, things could have been much worse, and I tried to give Luca that perspective. It was going to be a process, though. And he was just going to have to get through it.

He kept holding on to the hope that he would come back midway through the season. But the fact is that skull fractures, even minor ones like he experienced, take four to six months to fully heal. He had to come to grips with that reality, which wasn't easy.

Every fatherly tool I had was brought to bear, but it wasn't really having an impact.

As soon as Luca was cleared to start training again, I was on him to do just that. It wasn't happening. He didn't miss a practice, or a game, and he was leading from the sideline in every way he could, but he wasn't training. He just wasn't in an emotional place to do it.

Finally, Alexander and I really got hard on his ass about it, and he responded emotionally. Luca tends to keep things close to the vest. Alexander wears his emotions on his sleeve. Not

Luca. He expressed that he felt physically 100 percent, so it really tortured him that he couldn't play. He said that lifting made him feel even stronger, but more frustrated that he couldn't get on the field. He then went to his room. I waited for a few minutes, and then went up to talk to him. He was still crying, but I got him to gather himself. I told him that I appreciated and understood that he had to go through his emotional process and deal with the loss, but I wouldn't accept him feeling sorry for himself. I wasn't going to tolerate him having a pity party. Nobody gives a shit about anyone who wants to sit around and wallow in their own misery. I said there's nothing inspiring in that; and in fact, it repels people. I reiterated that perspective is important, and that he had to keep this incident in perspective. He was lucky that nothing more serious had happened. This would just be a blip on the screen, a bump in the road. Nothing more.

I said, "Before you know it, the season will be behind you, and you'll be putting your uniform on for your first game as a junior. This is a test of your character, and I know you have enough of it to get yourself back on track."

I told him I loved him, hugged him, kissed him, and walked out the door.

The next morning, Cindy and I were standing in the kitchen when we heard Luca's bedroom door close. We looked toward the stairs to see Luca—not walking—but bounding down the stairs. We hadn't seen that in a while.

He came over to me, gave me a big hug, and said, "Thanks, Daddy."

Then he hugged Cindy, told us he loved us, and he was out the door. We just looked at each other knowingly. HE'S BACK. No thanks needed.

CHAPTER **19**

‖‖‖

Bold and Beautiful . . . and Blessed

M y life on TV has never been better. I've been on *The Bold and the Beautiful* for ten years, and it's an absolute dream job. Going to work and jumping into the life of my fictional family, the Spencers, can definitely make any of the "drama" I've described in this book a yawn. No sleeping with my wife's sister. No sleeping with my son's wife. I haven't blown up one building, or been punched in the face by any of my boys.

I take a lot of pride in Bill Spencer Jr.'s success as a character spawning the Spencer dynasty. That doesn't happen without the incredible actors that I have as scene partners, and as such, a sister, a niece, wives, ex-wives, mistresses, children, nemeses, etc. You get the picture, and they all deserve props. My on-again, off-again wife Katie Logan, played by the incomparable Heather Tom; Bill's other ex-wife, who also happens to be Katie's sister [uh-huh], and the face of *B&B* since the first show aired, the one and only Katherine Kelly Lang, the past and current focus of Bill's intense love and affection, his daughter-in-law [don't judge], who's beauty is only surpassed by her talent, Jacqueline McInnis Wood, and Bill's sons Liam, Wyatt, and Will, played by wonderfully gifted Scott Clifton, Darin Brooks, and Zane Alexander Achor. And I can't leave out the bane of Bill's existence, Ridge Forrester, played by powerhouse Thorsten Kaye, or at the other end of the spectrum, Bill's right-hand man, confidant, and best friend, Justin Barber, played by the too cool, Aaron Spears.

Of course we can't do our jobs if we don't have scripts and the stories they tell, to bring to life. Those emanate from the mind of the best showrunner in daytime television, Mr. Bradley Bell. And what a team he has around him; cohead writers Michael Minnis and Mark Pinciotti, along with our outstanding scriptwriters.

We're all lucky to have our supervising producer, Ed Scott, and his discerning eye watching over our scenes from the booth. He directed my screen test for *The Young and the Restless* in 1984, and we're still together today. And they said it wouldn't last.

Our other supervising producer, Casey Kasprzyk, has an enthusiasm, love for the show, and creativity that's unmatched.

Our directing team of Cindy Popp (who's also one of our producers), Michael Stitch, Jennifer Howard, and Deveney Kelly have a passion for their craft and for the show that is on display every time they bring a script that lands on their desks to life. Every one of them is not only *technically* outstanding, but an actor's director with a collaborative nature, and all of us thespians respect and appreciate that.

The fact is that every person who works in every capacity and in every department on our show is an outstanding professional with a tremendous commitment to *The Bold and the Beautiful* and its success.

My ten years on *The Bold and the Beautiful* have gone by in the blink of an eye. The same with my years on *The Young and the Restless* and *Days of Our Lives,* which date back to 1984. In my personal life, I have more of a sense of the passage of time. So many markers, but the most revelatory one is that moment described earlier, when I first laid eyes on the woman that would become my wife. Cindy was THE ONE. It would take a while for that truth to come to fruition, but that feeling that I had when I saw her was right and true, and that has only been reinforced with time. I look at her across a room today and it's like laying eyes on her for the first time. It's a special feeling to still be enamored of this incredible woman twenty-one years later. I don't take it for granted. So beautiful, an amazing mom, wife, and professional. And she puts up with me. Saint!

In meeting Cindy, I broke a pattern. She didn't need rescuing or saving. She wasn't broken, so I didn't need to fix her. Just to love her.

When Cindy came into my life, she made me a better dad, a

better husband, a better actor, a better everything. More important than any of that, she made us a better family.

The days of having seven boys in the house are behind us. Four feels like a walk in the park.

Drew's married now and living in Texas. He's got an adorable son named Remy and another one on the way. Though he got his master's degree in architecture, he's decided not to pursue a career in that field, and instead is trying to make his way in the real estate business.

Lauren has an entrepreneurial spirit, and I really admire how much passion he has for his various creative pursuits. Currently, he's working in production and has started his own company, called Levels. He's producing commercials, music videos, branded content, and live events.

I am so proud of the man that Sasha has become. Those teenage years were tough, but he came out on the other side of them a better man. He taught himself about solar energy storage, and has created his own company, called Alumina Solar. He's single-minded in his pursuit of his company's success, and Cindy and I so admire his dedication.

Alexander recently graduated from IU in three and a half years with a degree in telecommunications. He had another year of football eligibility, but felt that as a quarterback he had accomplished everything he had set out to do, and had physically taken enough punishment. Cindy and I wholeheartedly agreed. He not only left Indiana as a fan favorite, but owning the record for the longest rushing touchdown by a quarterback in Indiana history: seventy-nine yards against the national champion Ohio State Buckeyes. He was also instrumental in IU's undefeated record against archrival Purdue during his career. Welcome to the real world, Alexander.

Luca just turned seventeen, is training his ass off, and is excited to get back on the football field to lead the Venice Gondos. He's killing it academically with a 4.2 GPA, and, oh yeah, did I mention that he's still finding time for the ladies?!?

Big Anton is loving ninth grade at Brentwood, and firing on all cylinders academically, athletically, and socially. It's basketball season, and the Tank, or BamBam, which are my nicknames for him, is owning the paint. We just got back from Mexico, and boogying BamBam was bustin' some moves on the dance floor. Not really, but we're working on it.

Davis transitioned from a very small private school to very large Palisades High. It was a really challenging transition to go from such an intimate environment to a high school with a student body of about three thousand kids. It was a bumpy start, but he rose to the occasion and is killing it. He's made a bunch of new friends, and he's getting it done in the classroom and on the hard court. He made the basketball team in a highly competitive tryout and like his twin, Curly—yep, that's my nickname for him—is blocking shots on defense and a force to be reckoned with on the offensive side.

All of our boys have their own special character traits and

unique personalities, but a common thread that runs through all of them is the joy of breaking Daddy's balls. I guess that definitely gets passed on through the generations, because I used to like to do the same thing to my dad.

⁗⁗⁗⁗⁗⁗⁗⁗⁗⁗

In Alexander's first year in Bloomington, he met a teammate, Ty Smith, who would become his best friend. I call him Country. What can I say, I'm a nicknamer. Cindy and I became friends with Ty's parents, Tracy and Jaime. Tracy Smith was the Hoosiers' head baseball coach for years, leading them to the College World Series before taking the head coaching job for the Arizona State Sun Devils. During spring break in 2016, Tracy invited me to throw out the first pitch at an Arizona game. We decided to make a family vacation out of the trip and bring all of the boys. We had a blast, which included getting in a round of golf.

Cindy loves golf. And she's good at it. Did I mention she's also competitive? Did I mention I'm competitive? Wife competitive + husband competitive + golf = $!&(^$)(@^#*%. Do the math! That's why I let her win.

Yeah, not true. She kicks my ass.

One ass whooping was enough. Then it was my time to shine in the Sun Devils' stadium.

I was warming up with one of the players, and Coach Smith and my boys were trying to get in my head by giving me all sorts of crap, telling me I was going to choke.

"You're gonna throw a wild pitch."

"You're gonna throw it in the dirt."

"Old man this," and "Old man that." Blah, blah, blah.

I told them, "There'd have to be something IN MY HEAD for you to get at."

I'd already thrown out a first pitch at Camden Yards in front of 55,000 people, so this was going be a piece of cake. The number of Sun Devils fans certainly didn't match that of the Baltimore Orioles fans, but they didn't have to. That night the stadium held the most important people in my life. I walked out to the mound and looked up, and there was the Sun Devils' catcher behind the plate. But in my mind's eye, I saw my dad popping the catcher's mitt with his fist; but at the same time, it was as though he was sitting on my shoulder, whispering in my ear.

"All right, Deeb. Show me what you got. Look at the target, but don't aim it. Just throw it."

And that's what I did. Fastball. Split the plate in half.

Thanks, Dad.

I hope as the boys go on in their lives, if they need me every now and then, they'll know that THEIR dad is sitting on their shoulder, just a whisper away.

ACKNOWLEDGMENTS

‖‖‖

Cindy and I were invited to a dinner party at the home of our dear friends Bob and Myrna Schlagel to celebrate Bob's sixty-fifth birthday. They are wonderfully fun and engaging people, and I anticipated us having a great time. I did not anticipate that attending that evening would result in my taking on the most daunting task in which I've ever been engaged: the writing of this book. I was seated next to an incredibly lovely, bright, charming, and dynamic woman by the name of Jan Miller. Turned out that Jan was the founder and CEO of the global literary agency Dupree Miller & Associates. They're well beyond a literary agency, but that's really beside the point. As we were initially engaging in conversation, and talking about our personal lives, I had no idea what Jan did for a living until I heard the fateful words: "You have to write a book!" Ha! Ha! Sure. That's outside my wheelhouse. Not something I have any interest in doing. Well, you might say that Jan has a way about her, and to cut to the chase she figuratively grabbed me by the scruff of my neck and here I am writing the acknowledgment section of…MY BOOK. Jan, you're one in a million. Thank you!

There are plenty of thank-you's to go around, and none more important, or meaningful, to me than my go-to agent, my supporter, my hand-holder, my advisor, and my friend, Senior Agent

Lacy Lalene Lynch. Thank you, Lacy. I wouldn't have gotten through this without you.

To my editorial director, Kate Hartson, thank you for believing in me, this book, and for your patience. To everyone else at Hachette, you have my gratitude and appreciation for your hard work and efforts to make this book a success:

Jaime Coyne, associate editor

Grace Johnson, assistant editor

Laini Brown, senior publicist

Patsy Jones, VP of marketing

Bob Castillo, senior managing editor

Molly Albert, production editor

Giraud Lorber, senior production manager

Jody Waldrup, art director

To *The Bold and the Beautiful's* Team Diamont, thank you, thank you, a thousand times, thank you:

Dustin P Smith, vice president of communications for CBS Entertainment

Eva Basler, vice president of communications for Bell-Phillip Television Productions, Inc., *The Bold and the Beautiful*

David Gregg, vice president of international publicity for Bell-Phillip Television Productions, Inc., *The Bold and the Beautiful*